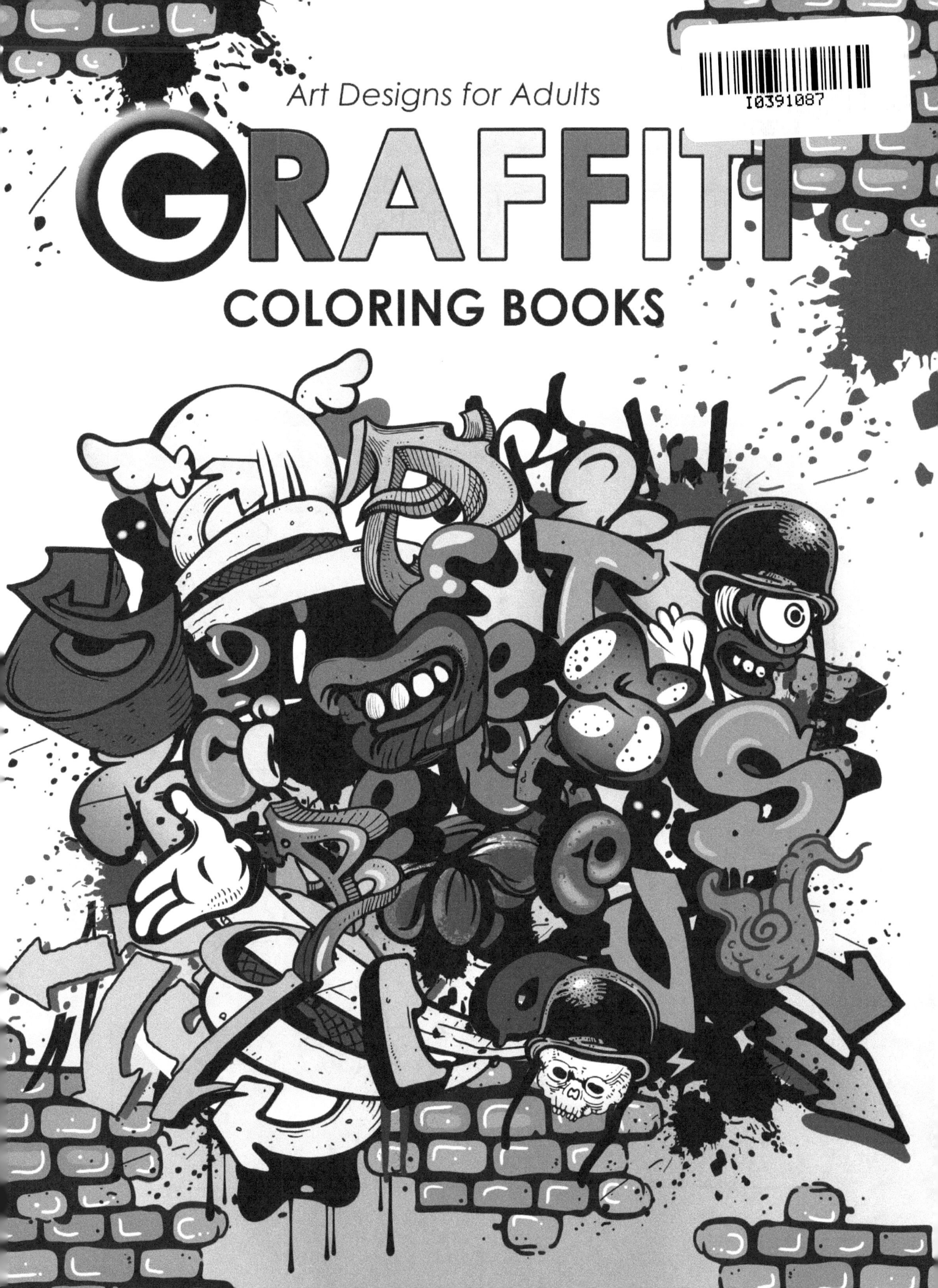

Art Designs for Adults

GRAFFITI

COLORING BOOKS

TEST YOUR COLOR

TEST YOUR COLOR

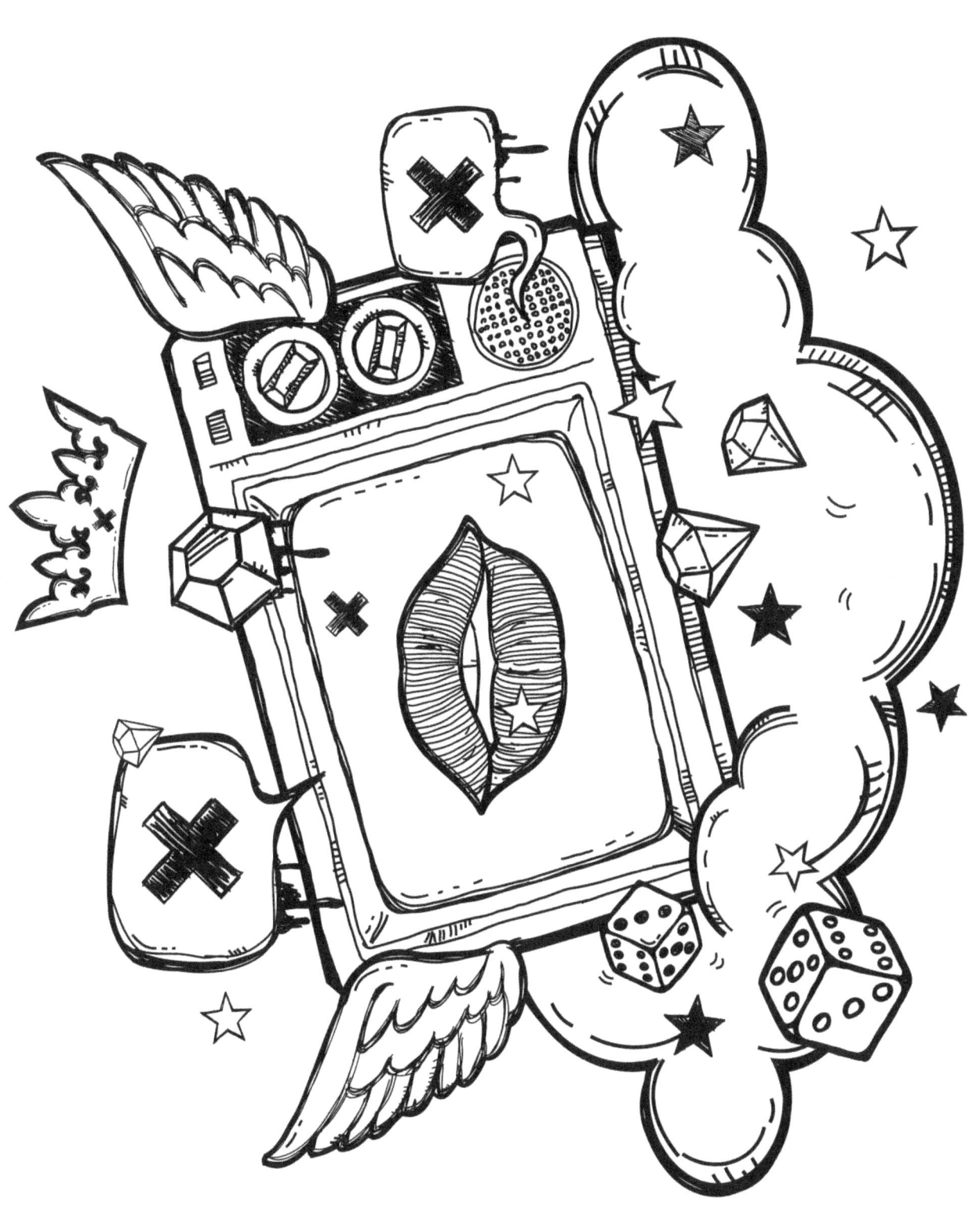

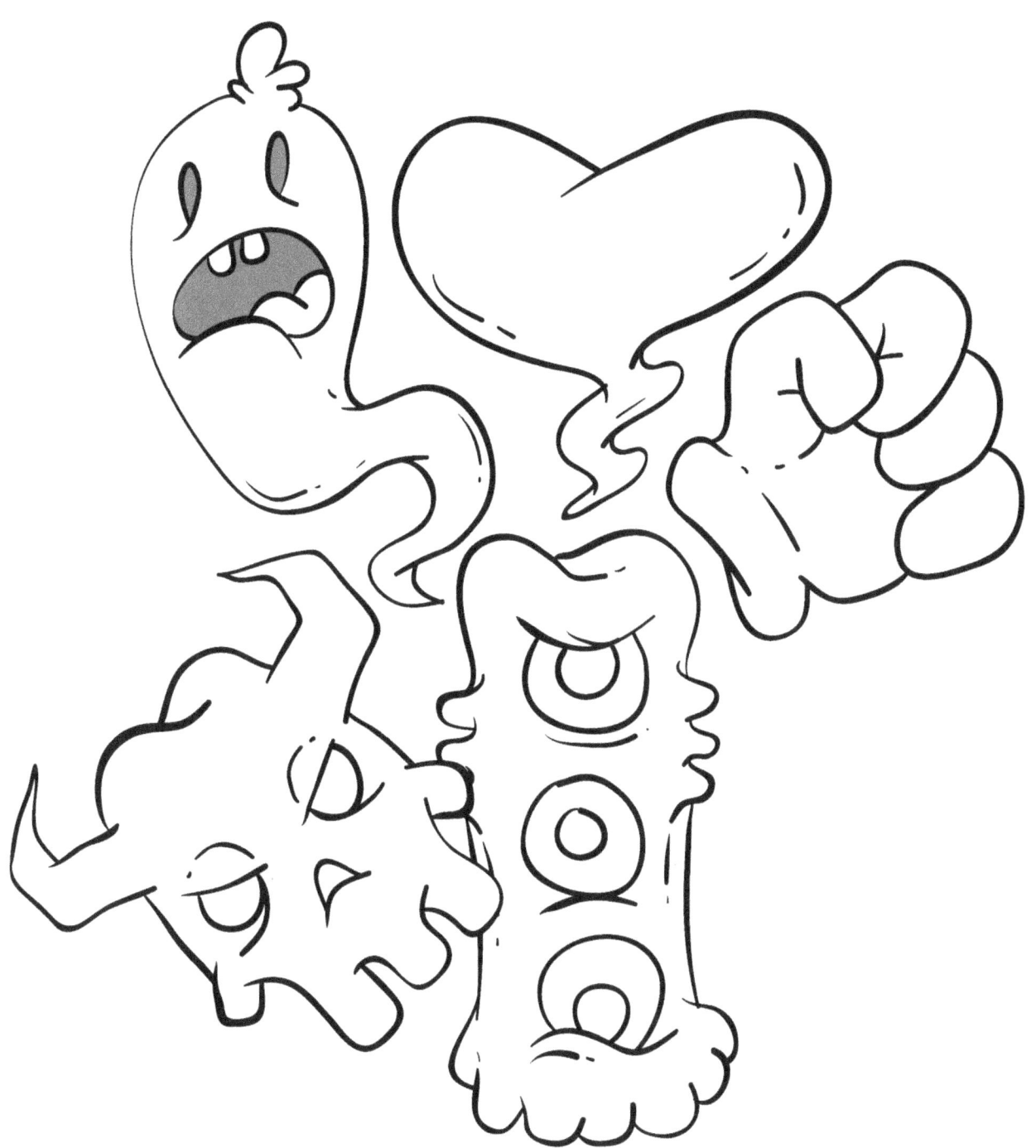

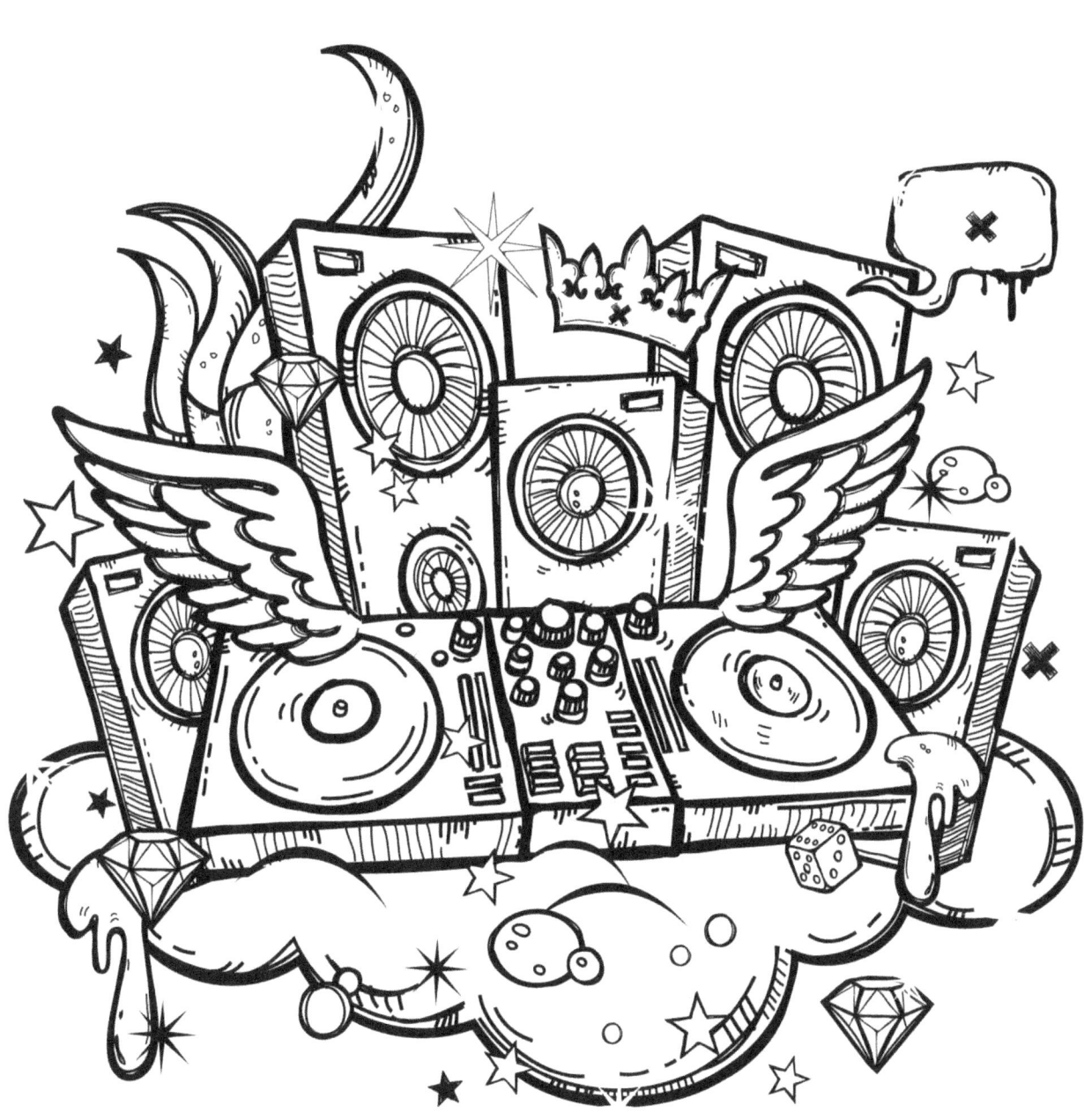

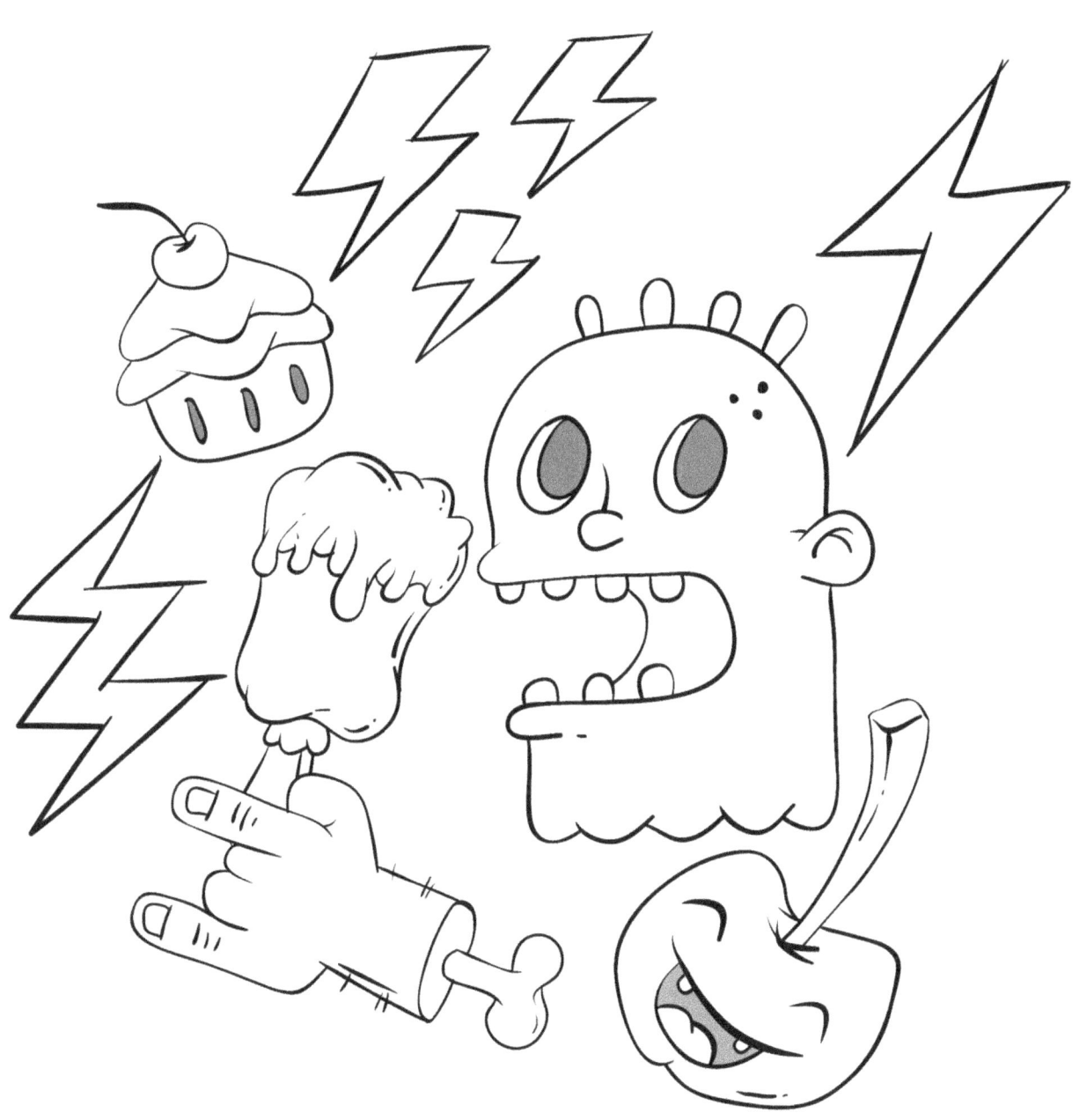

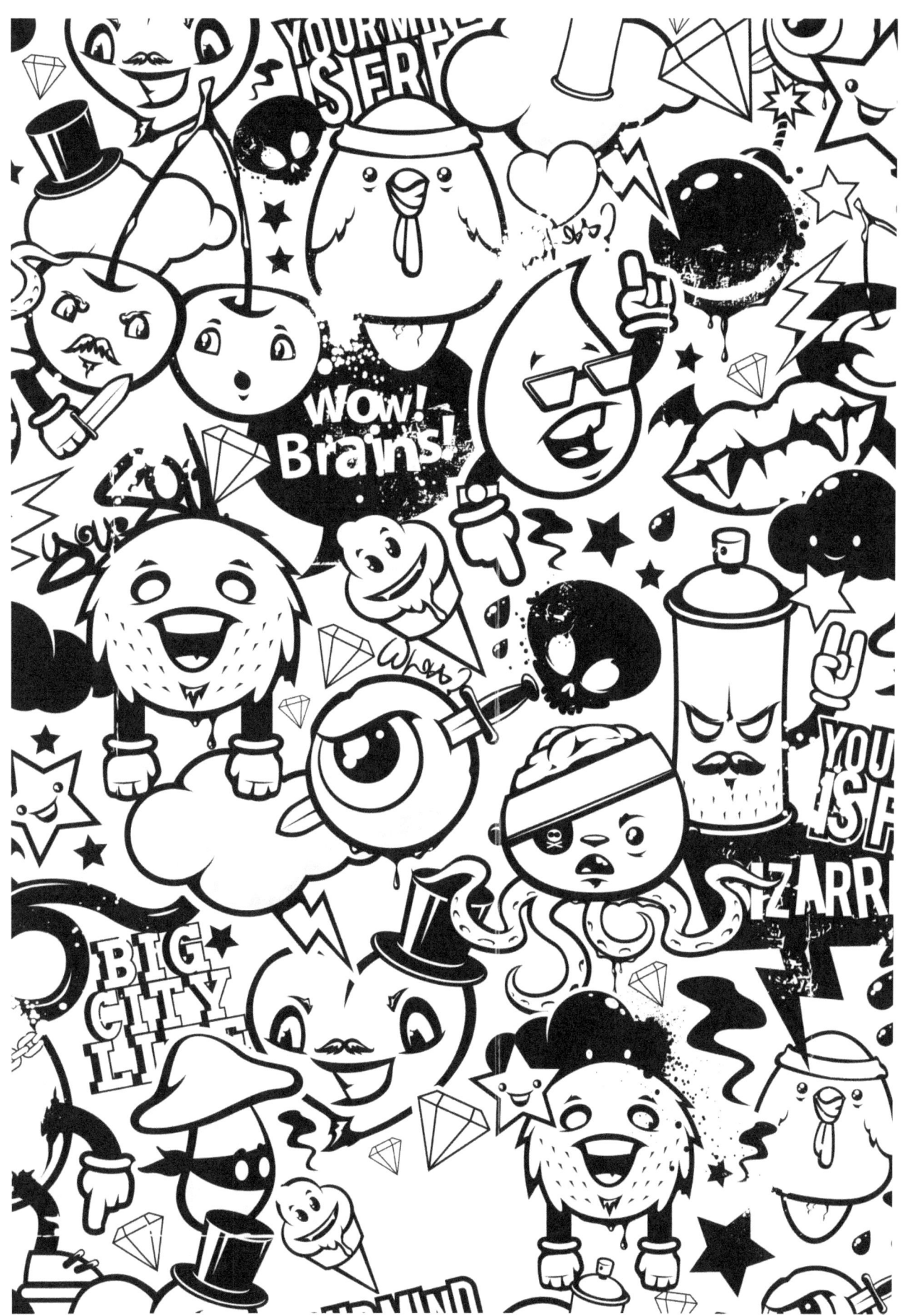

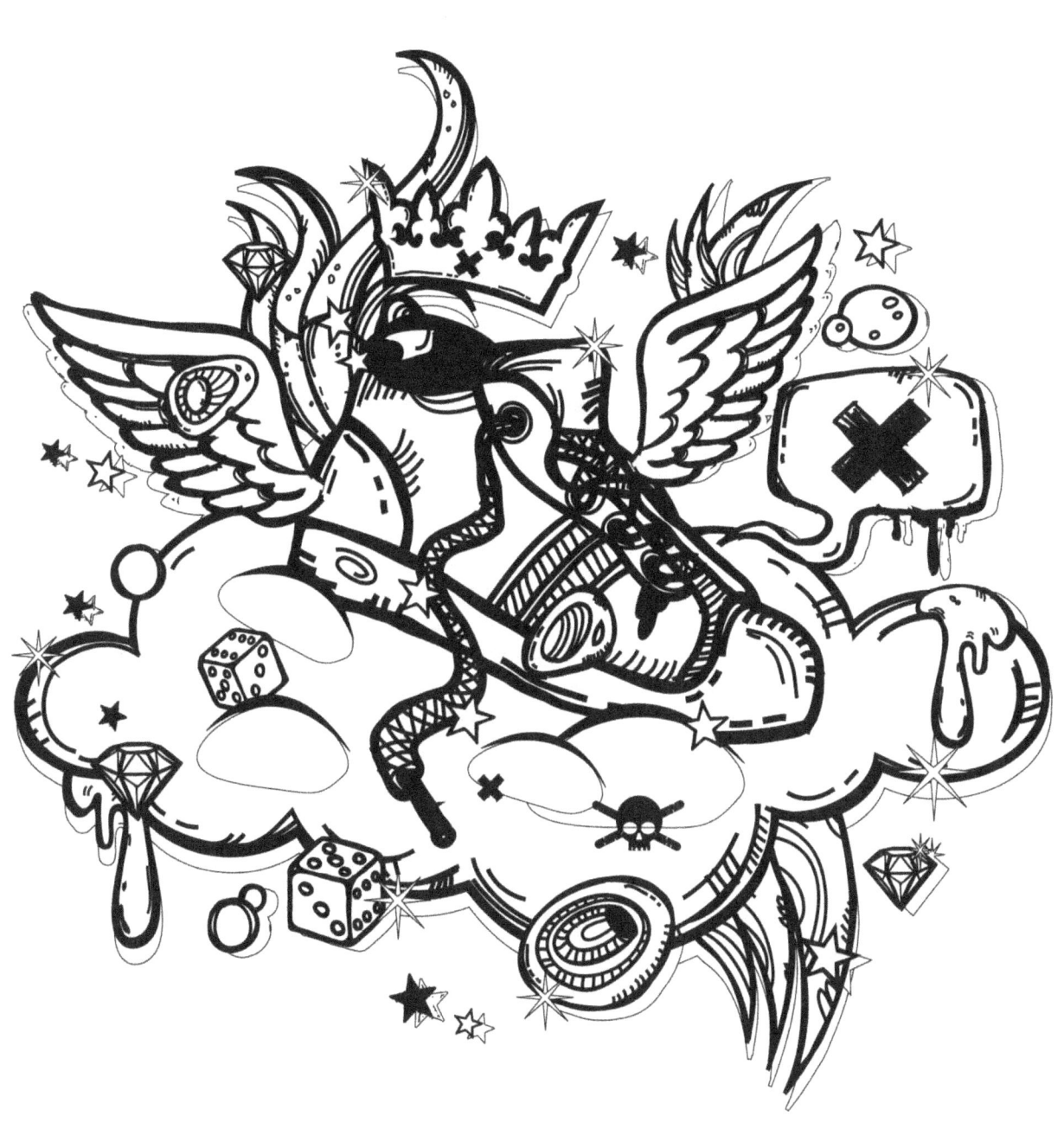

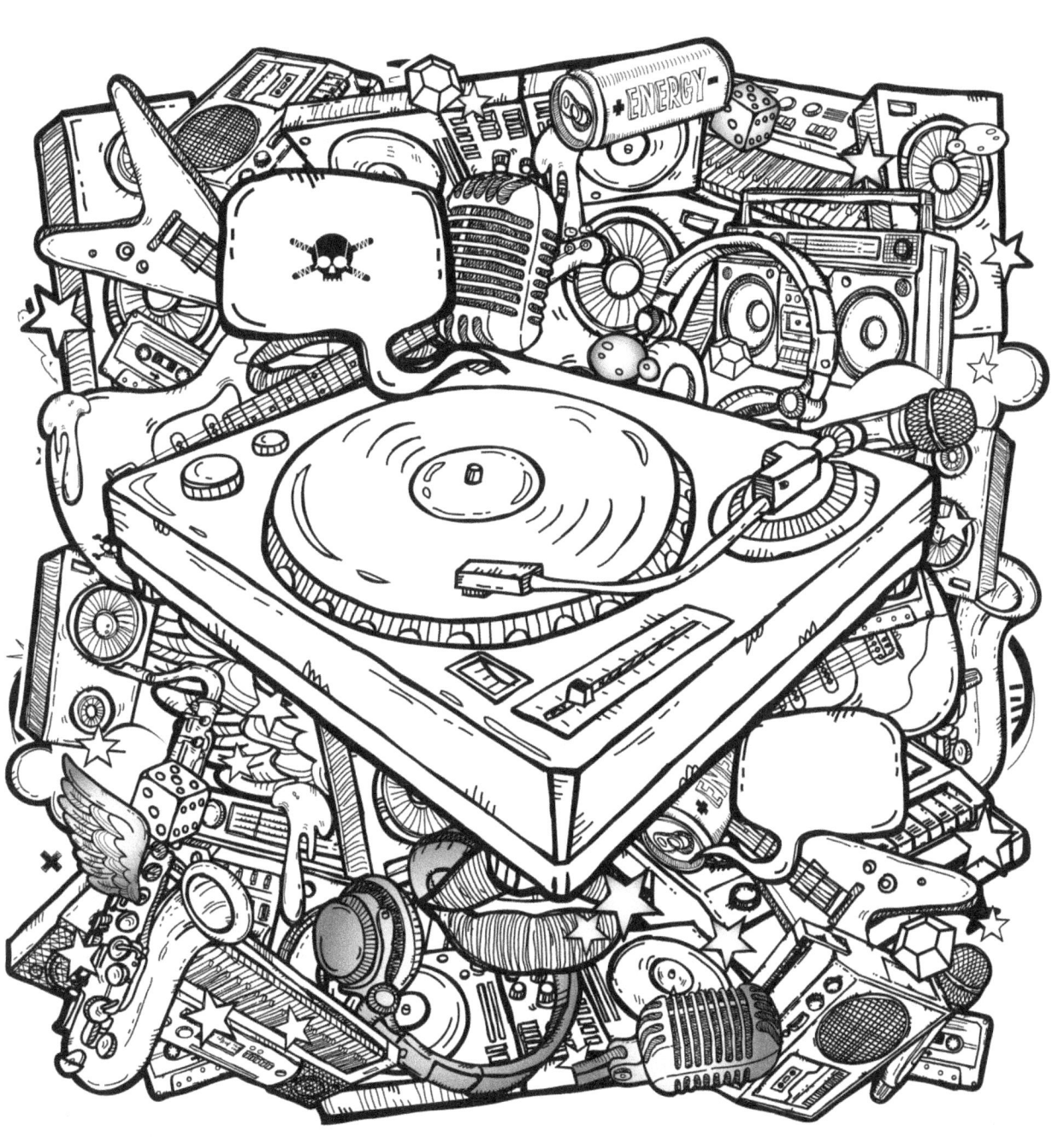

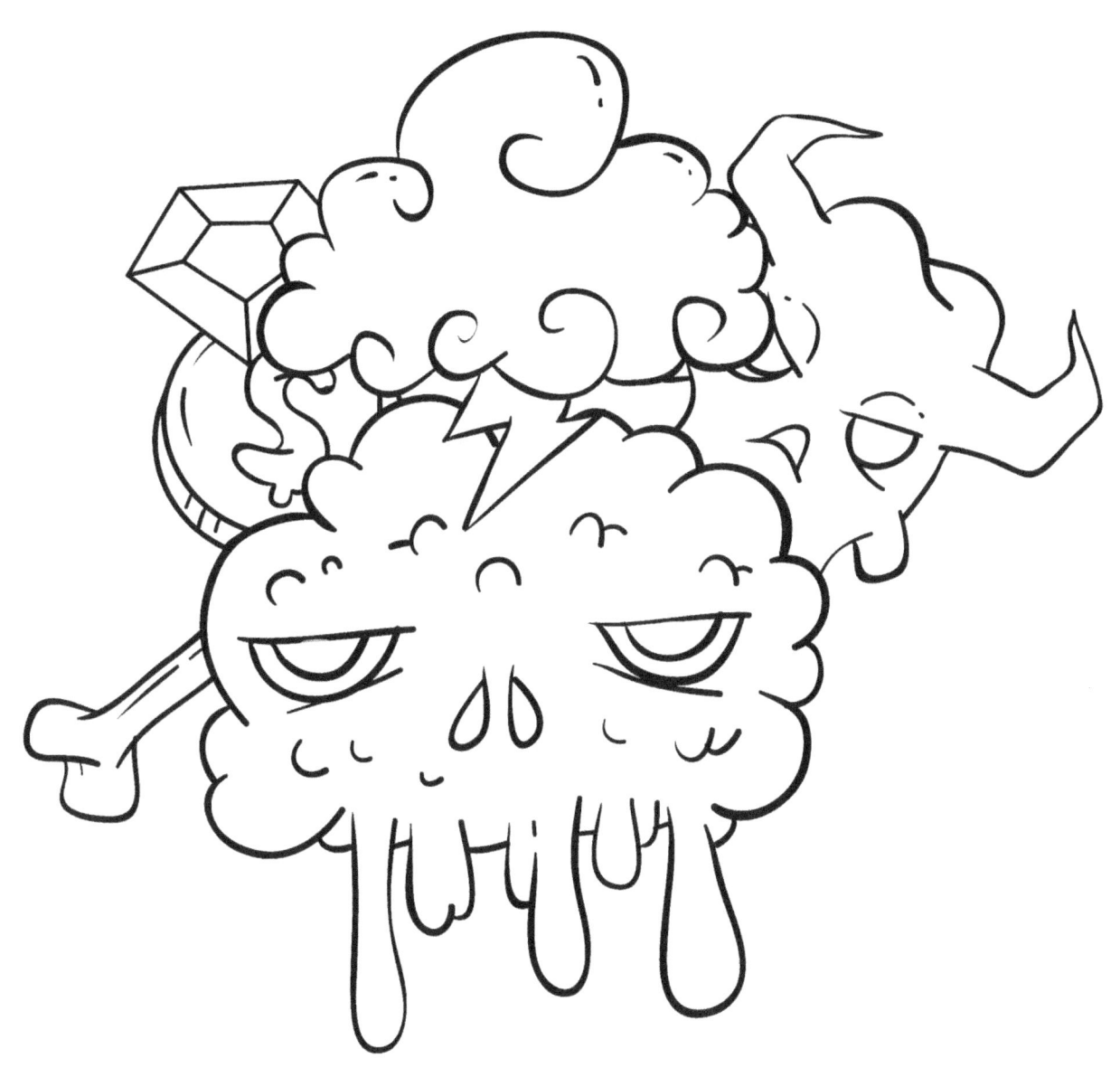

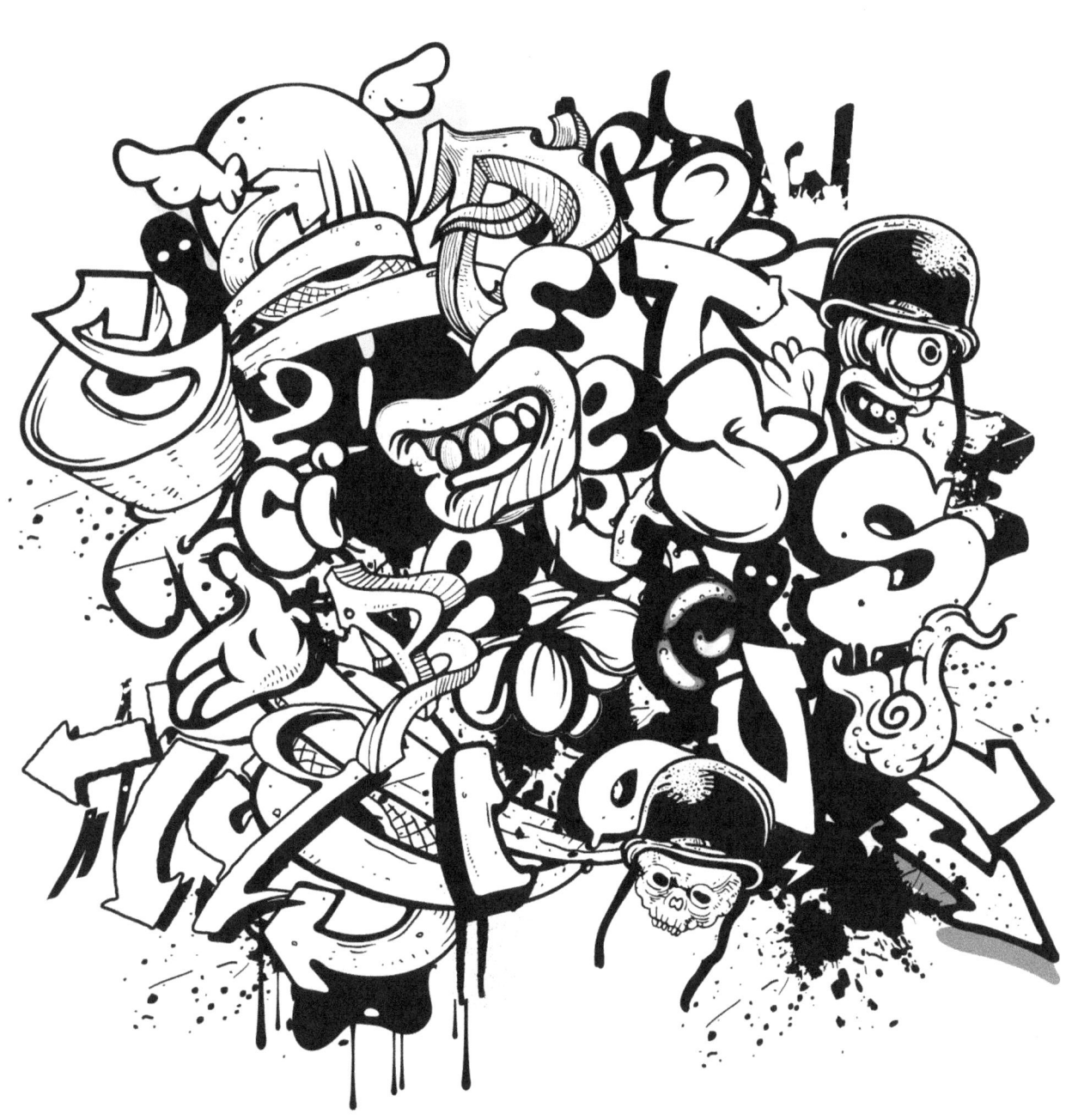

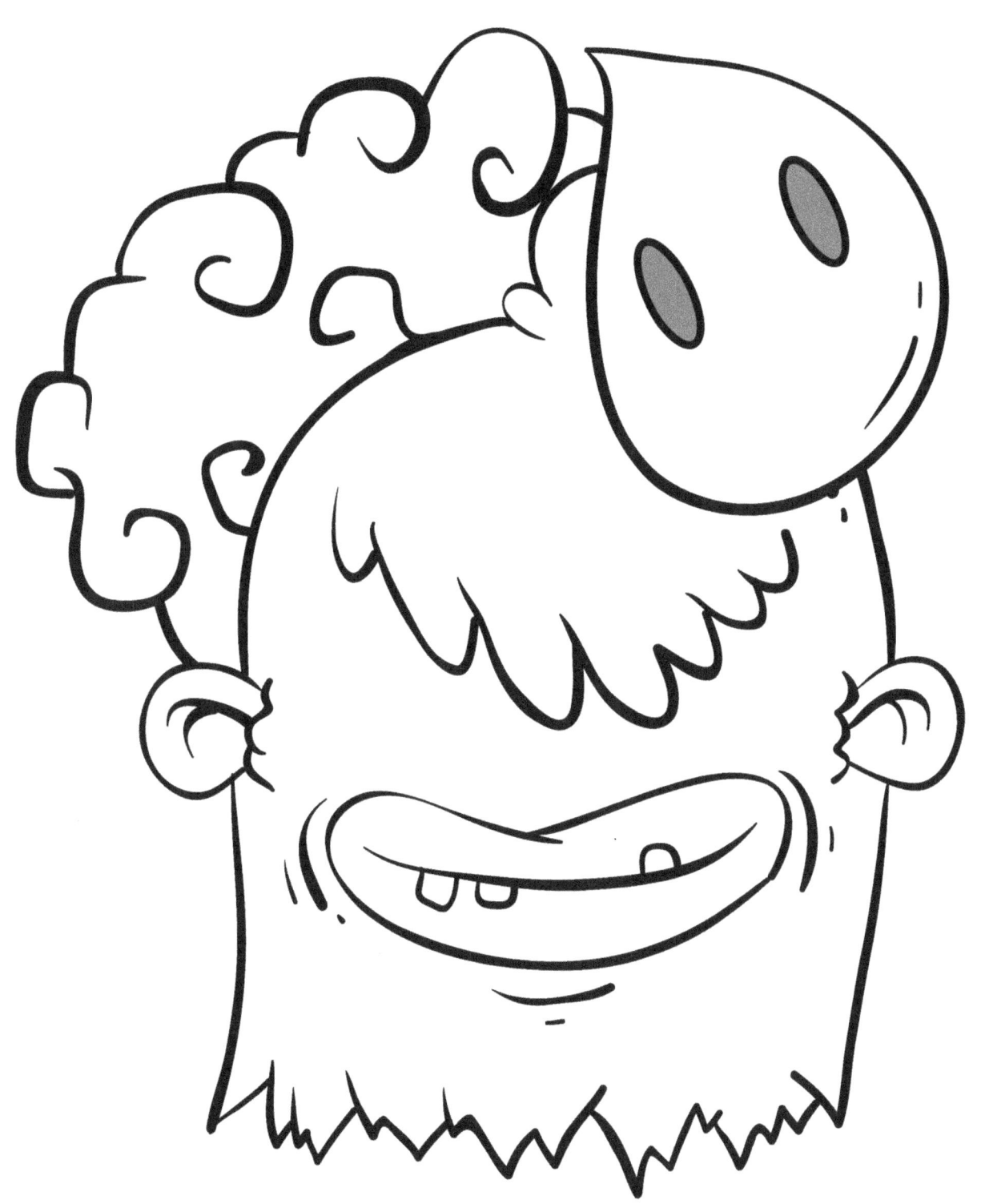

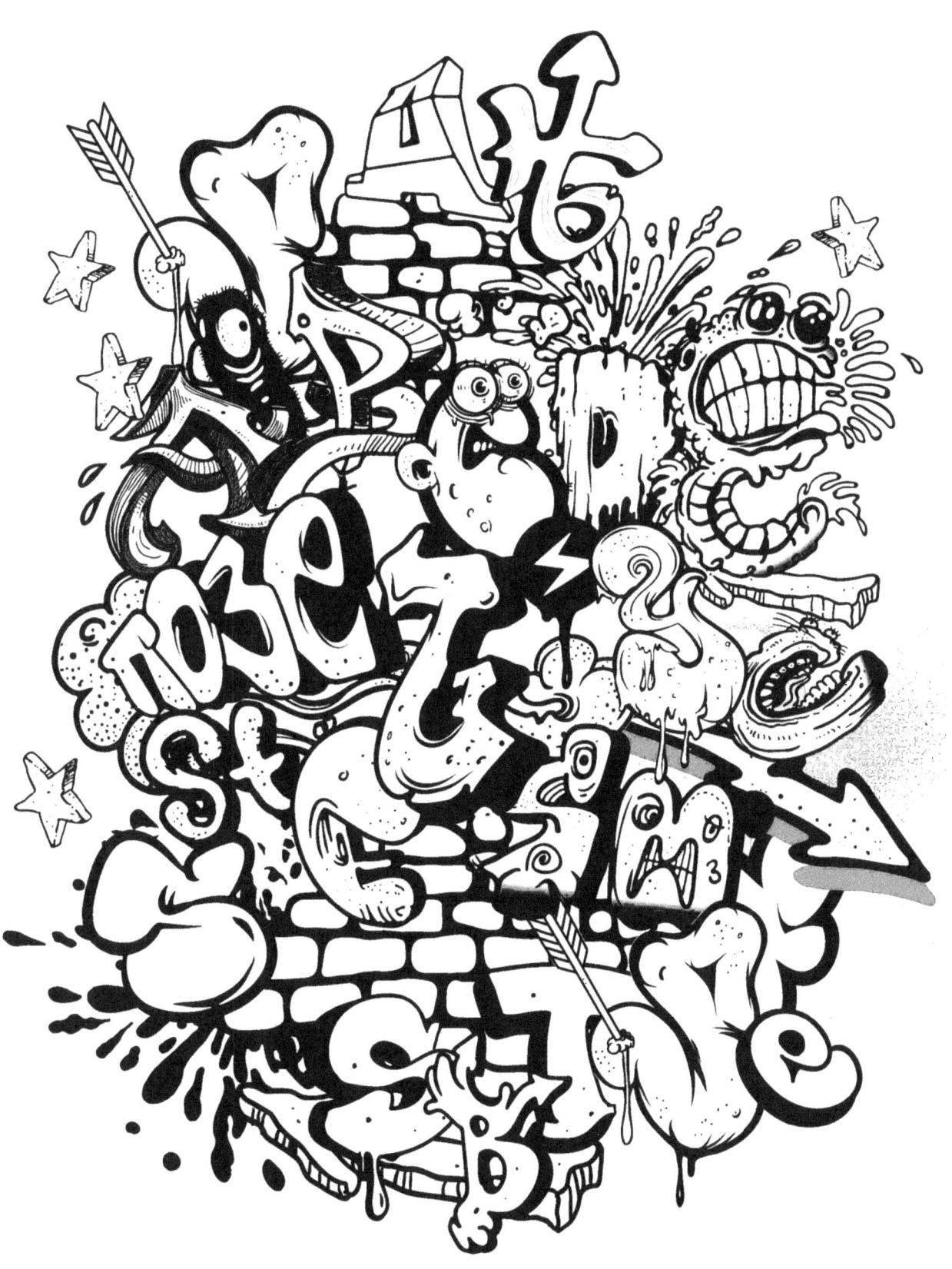

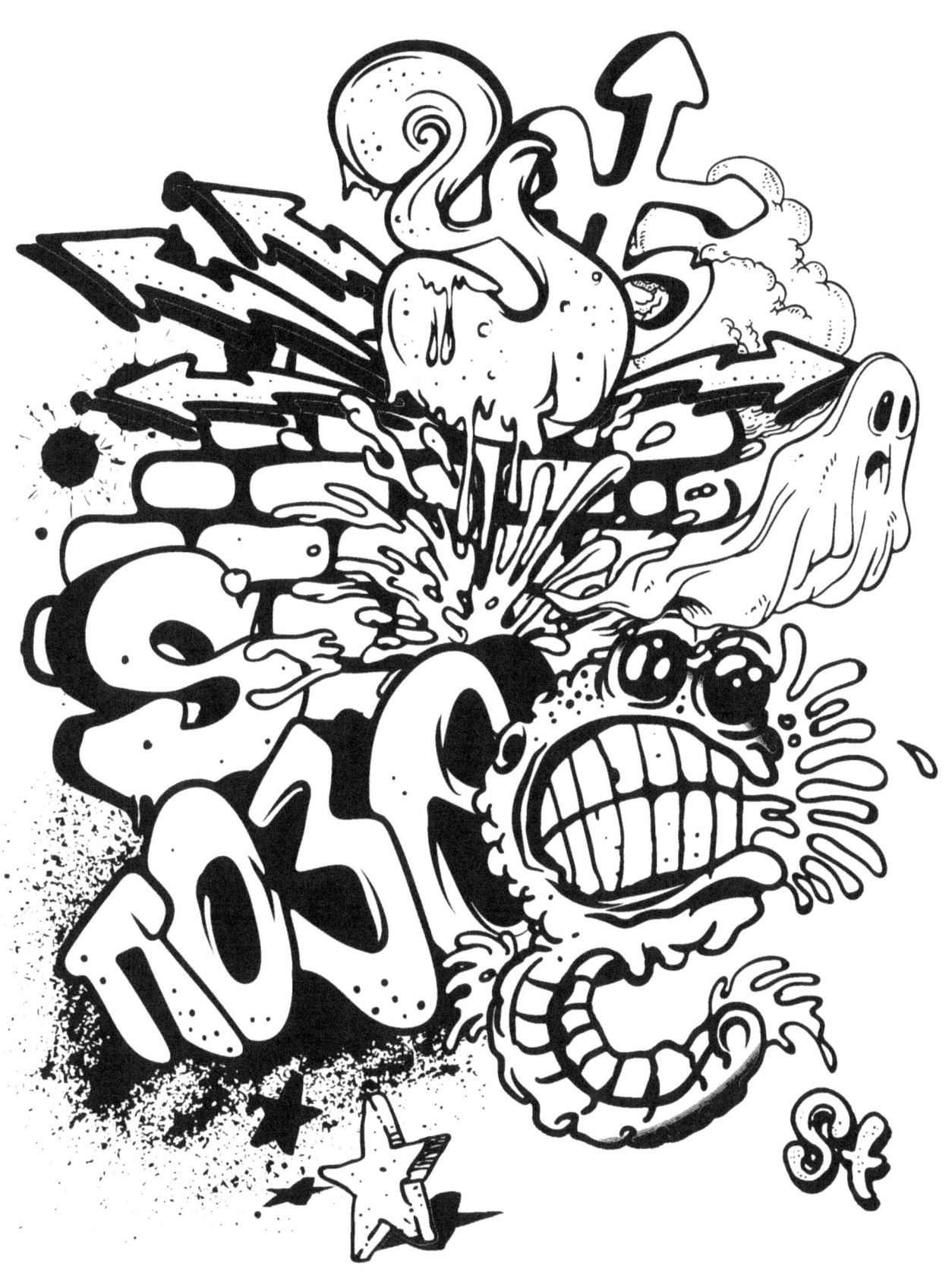

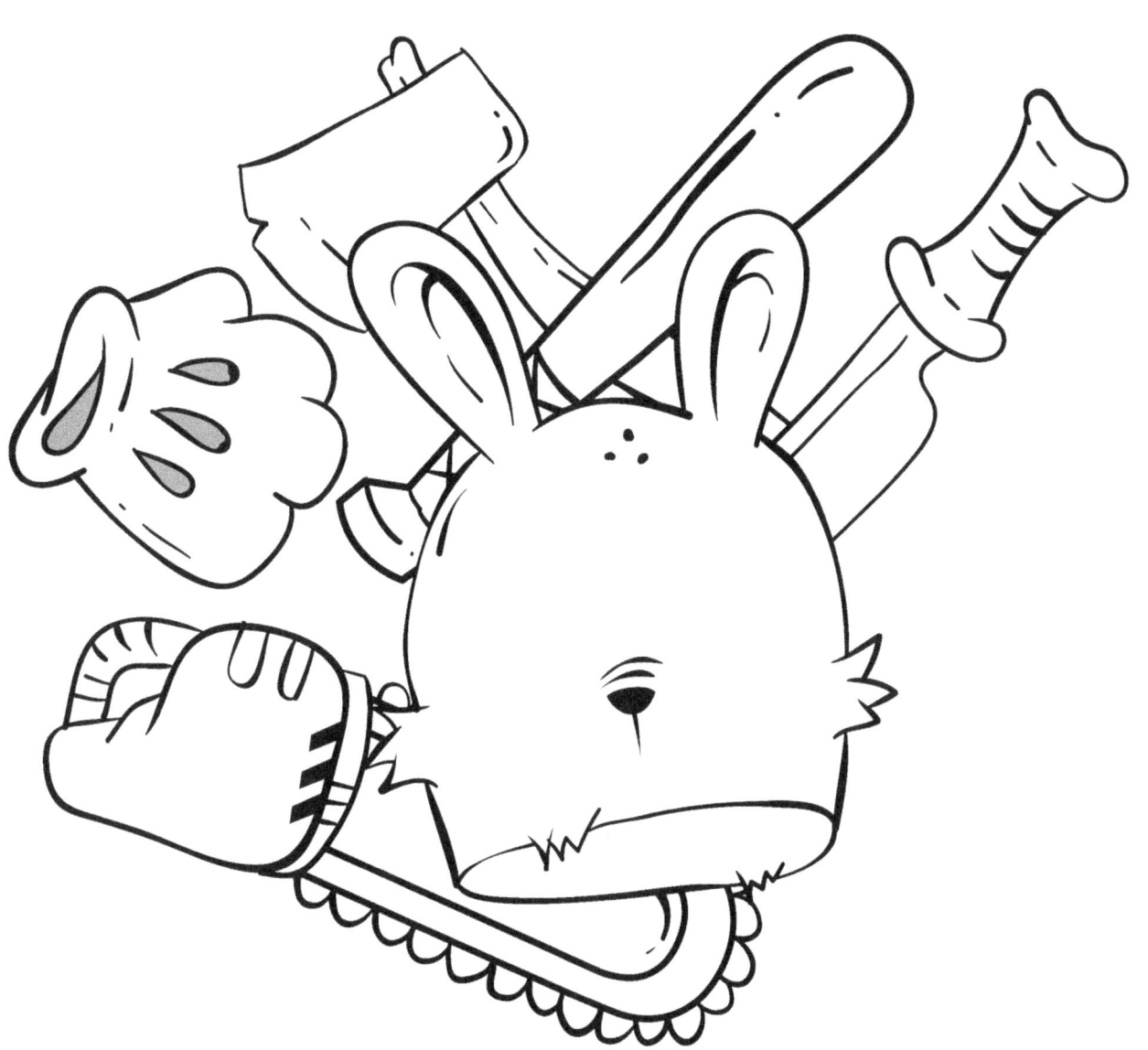

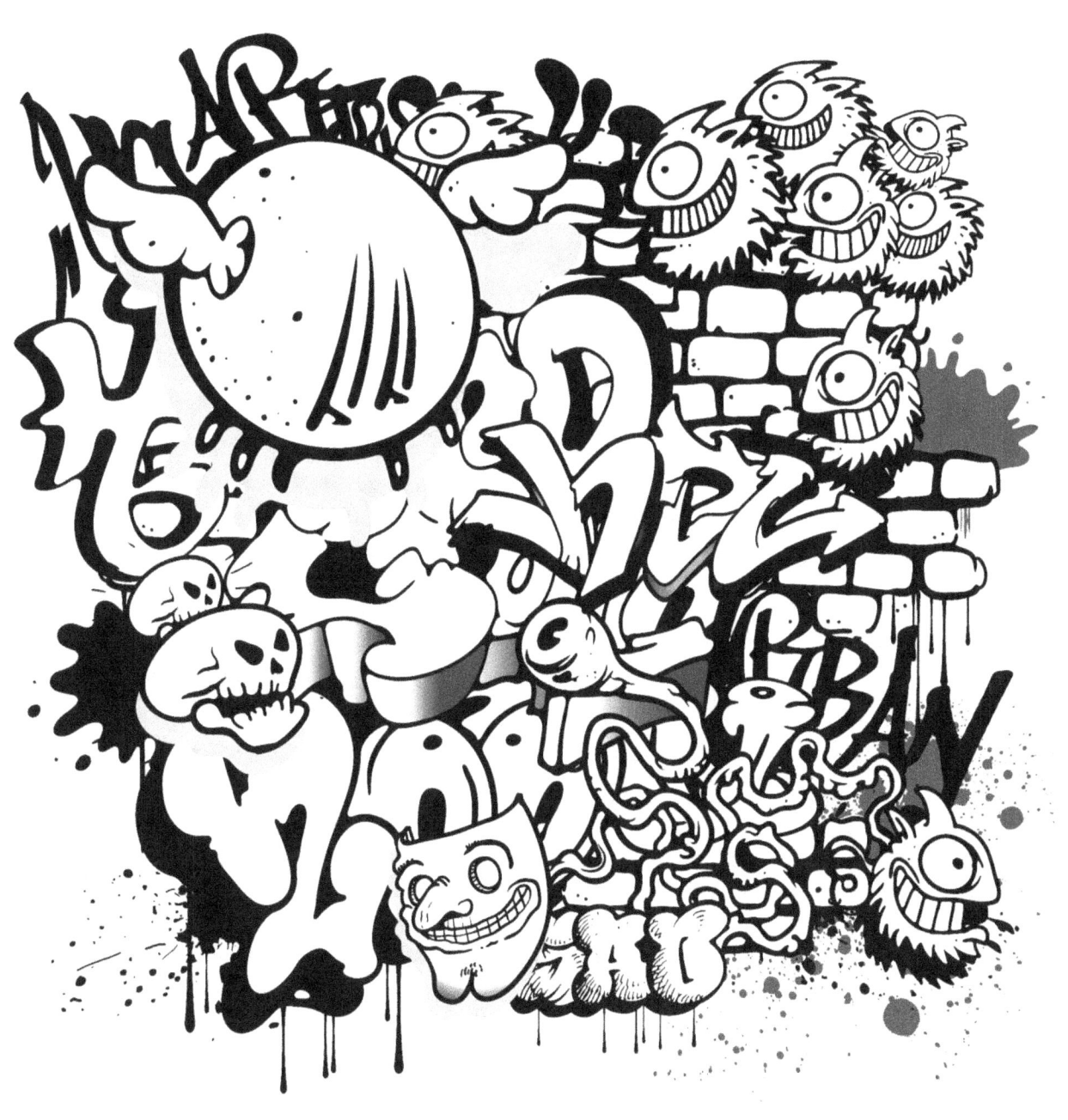

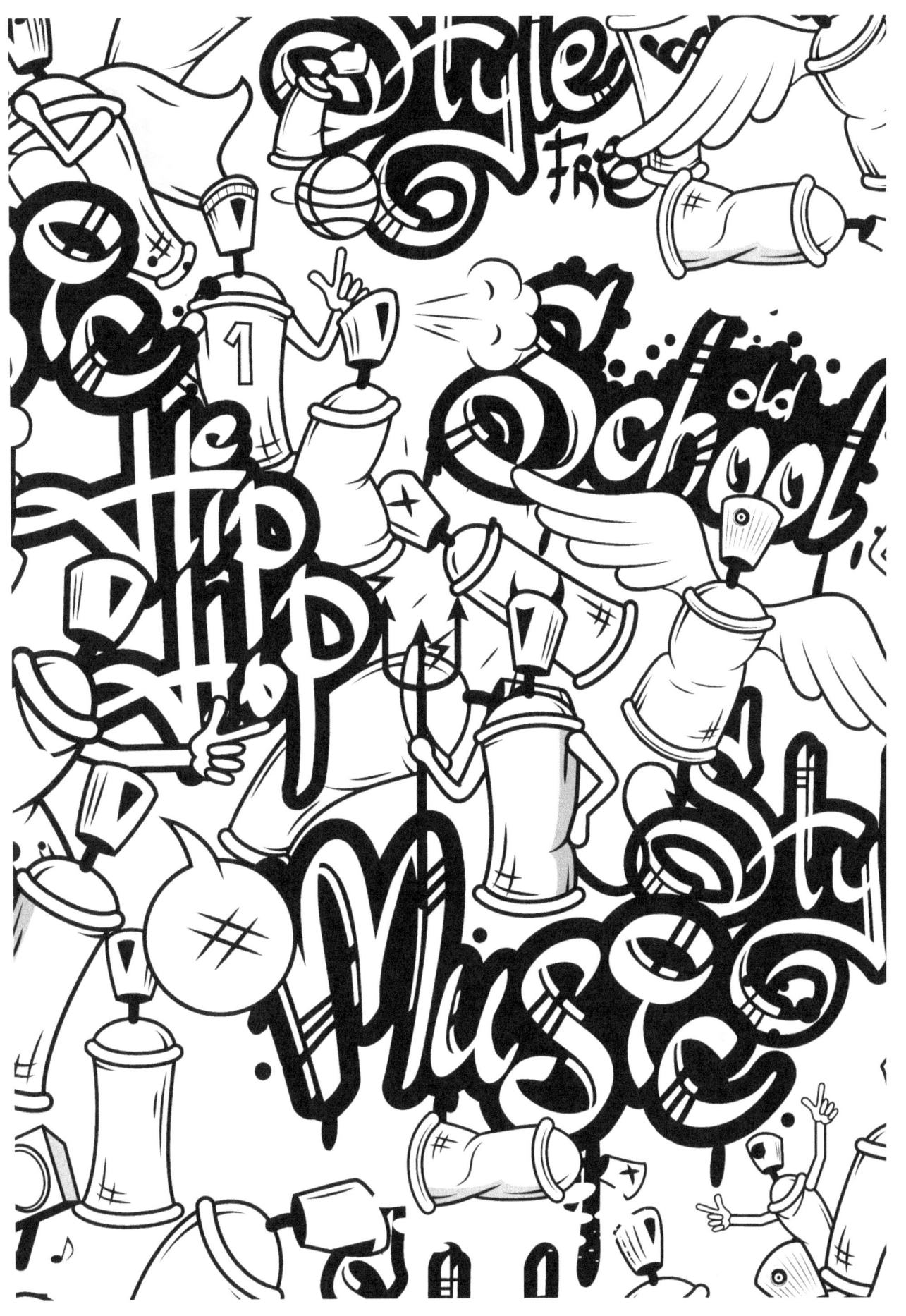

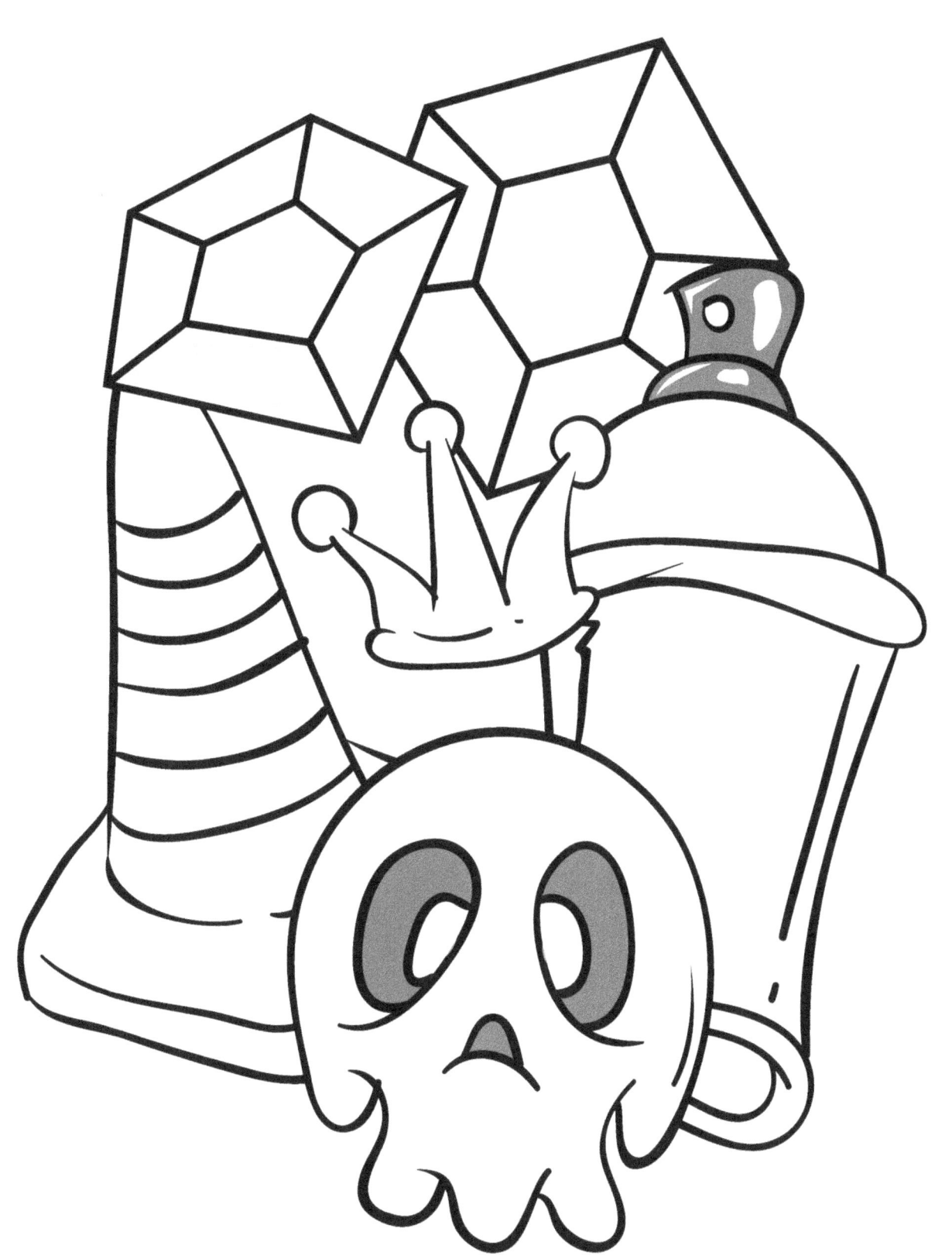

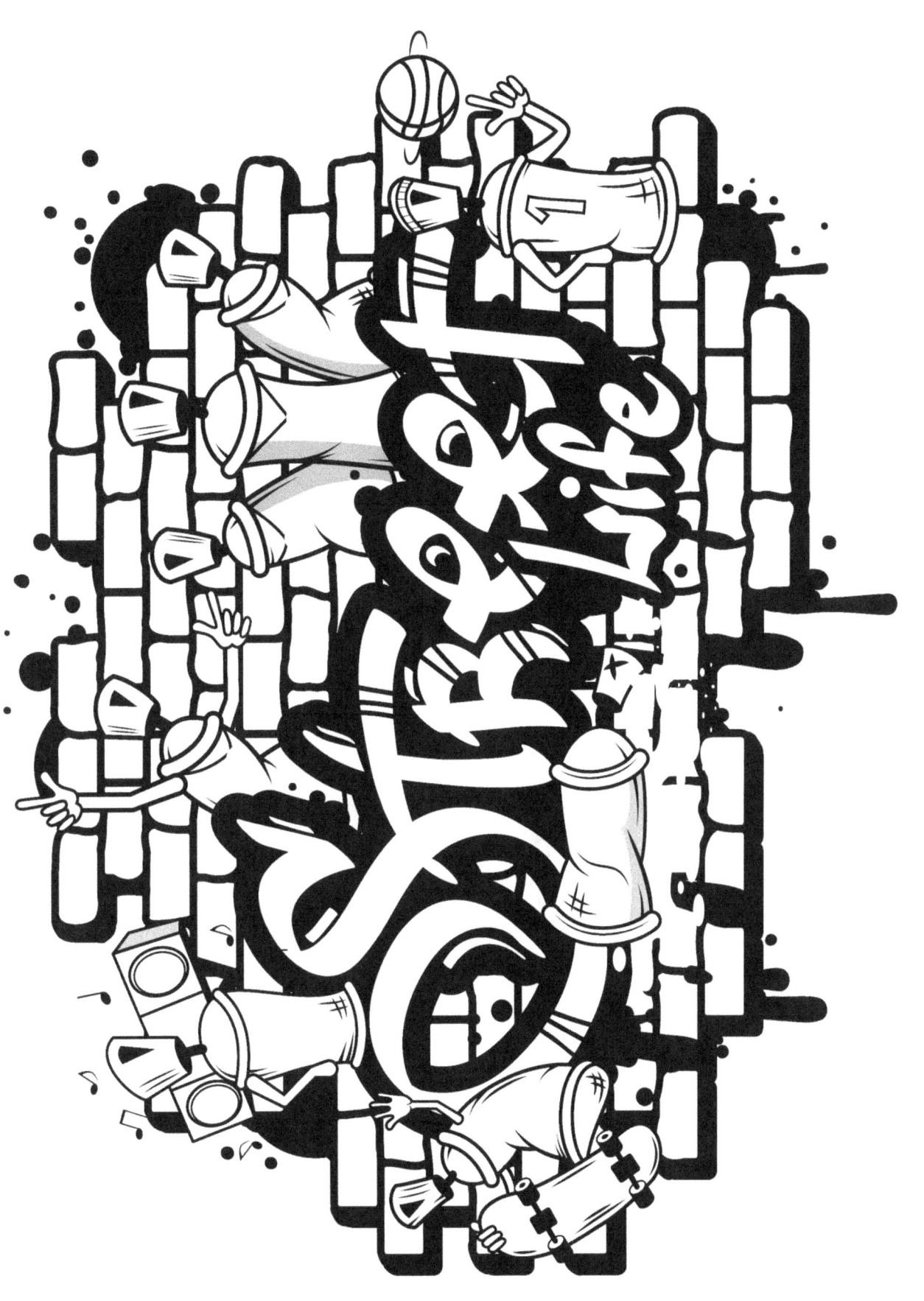

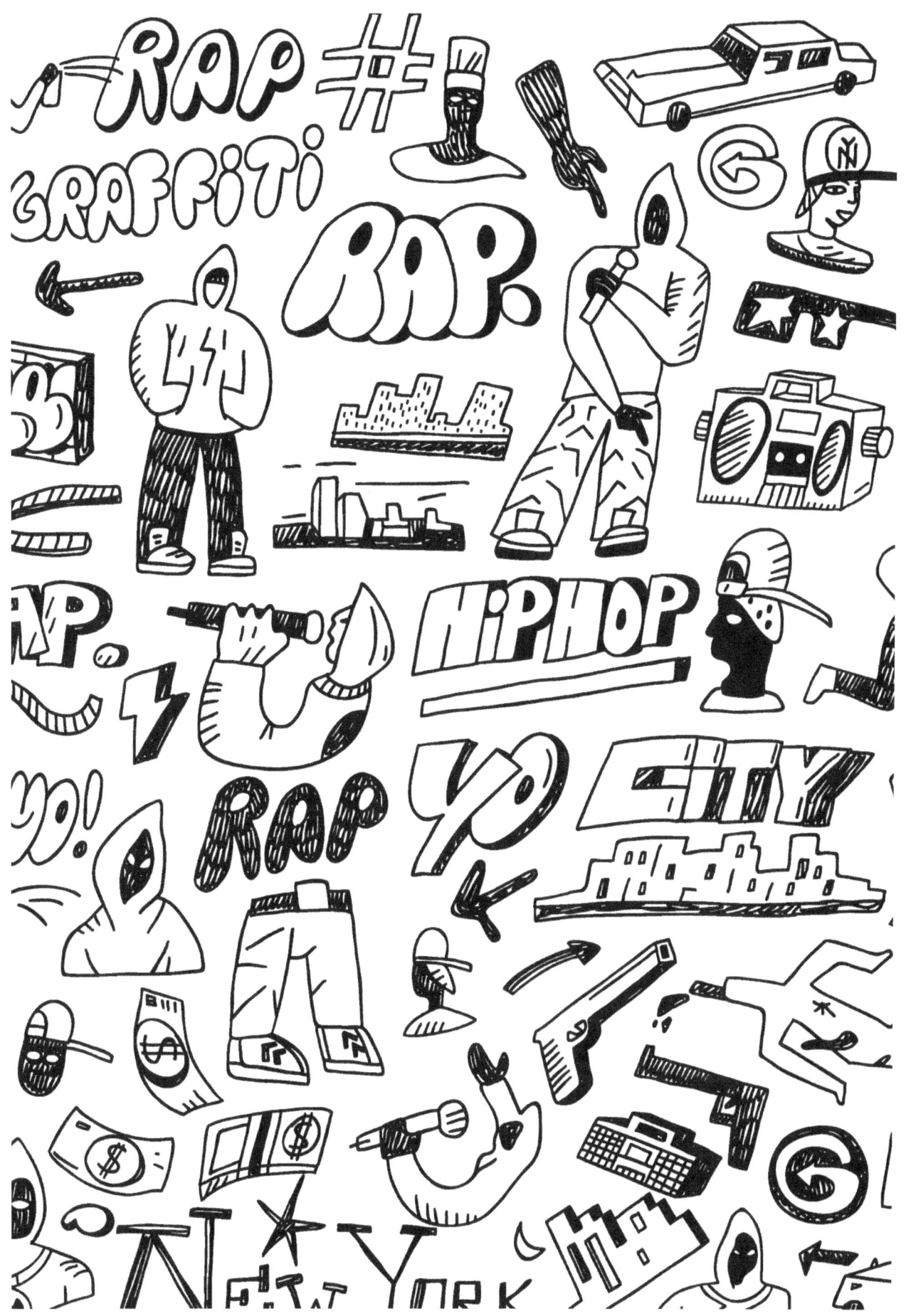

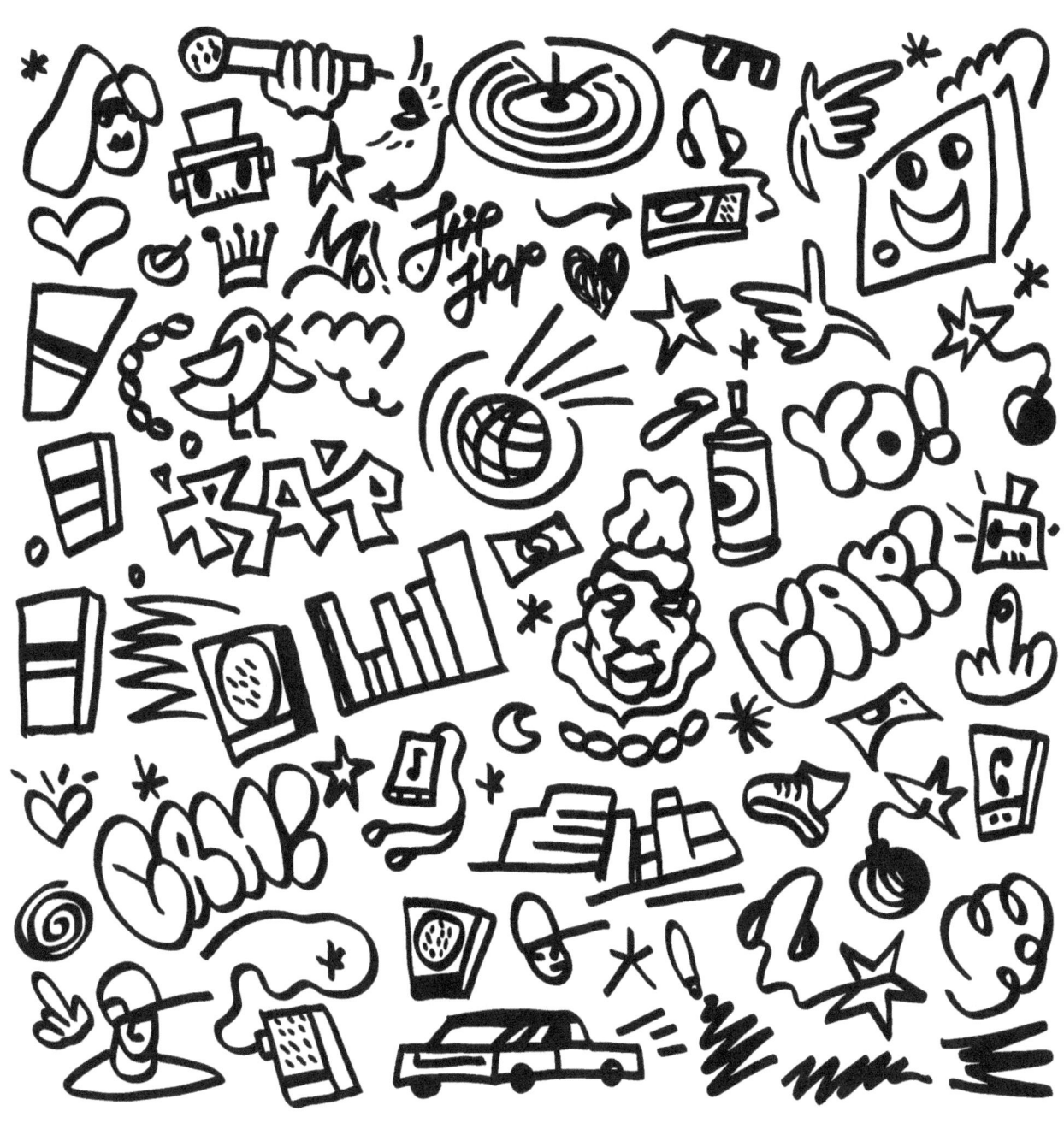

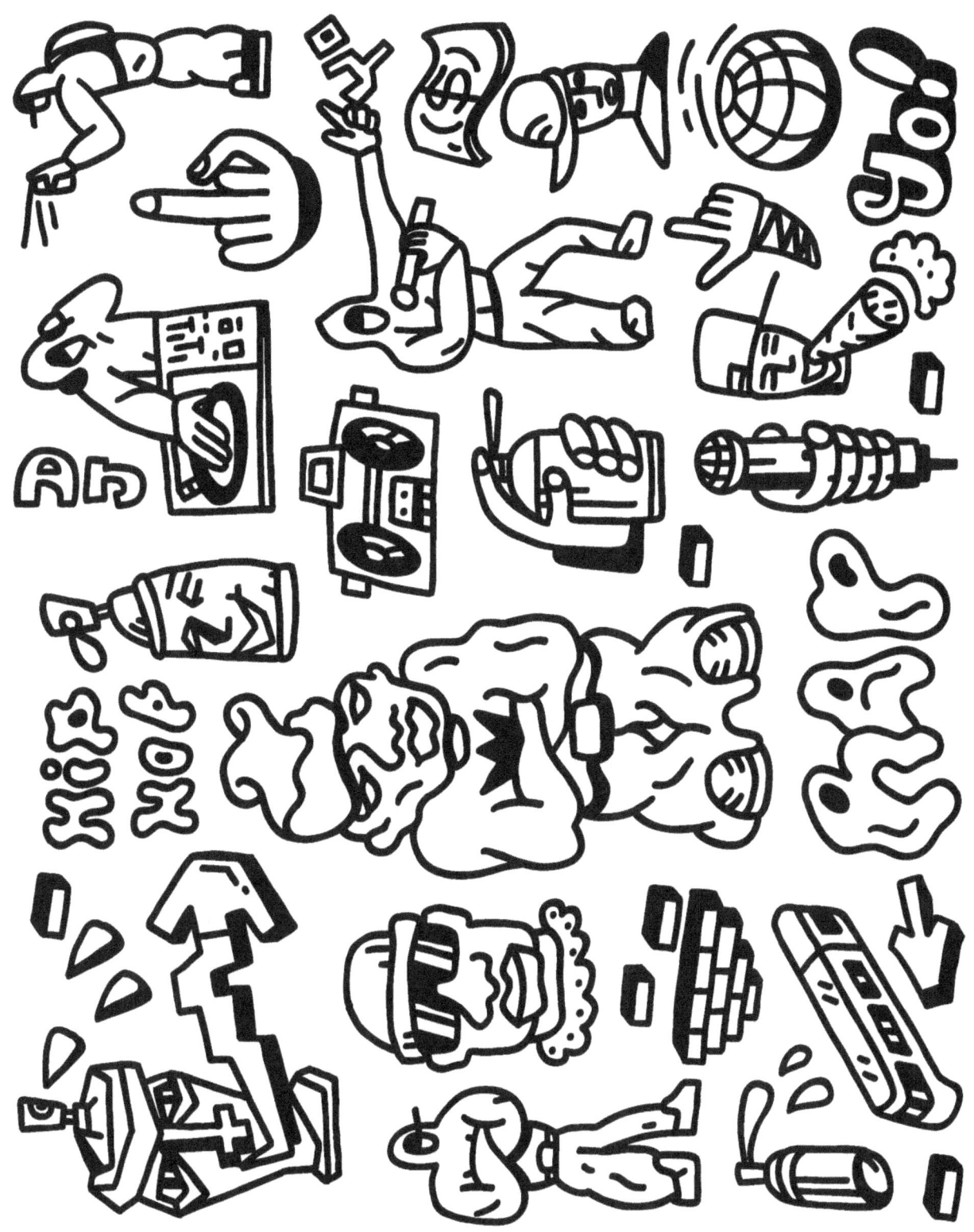

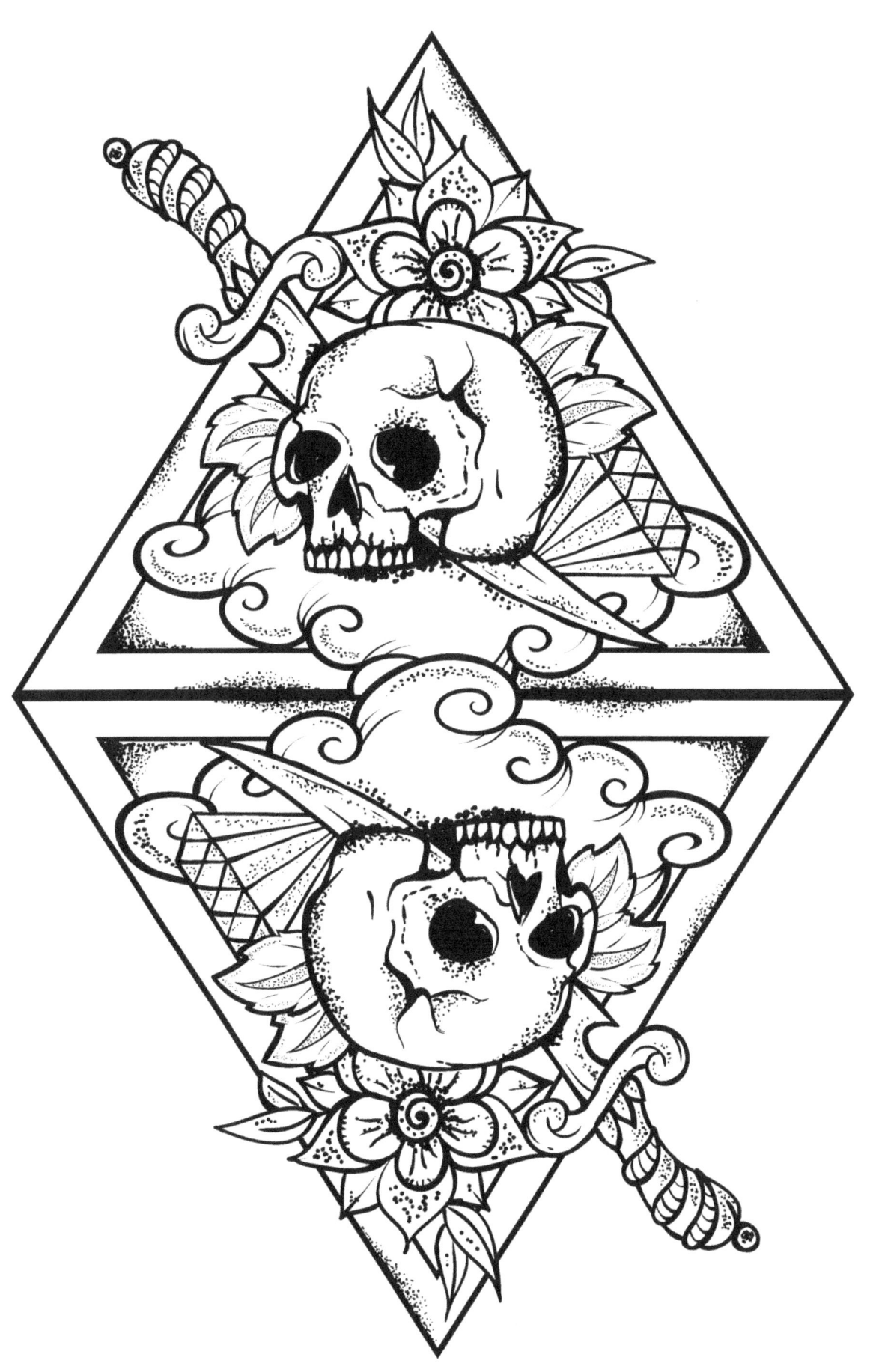

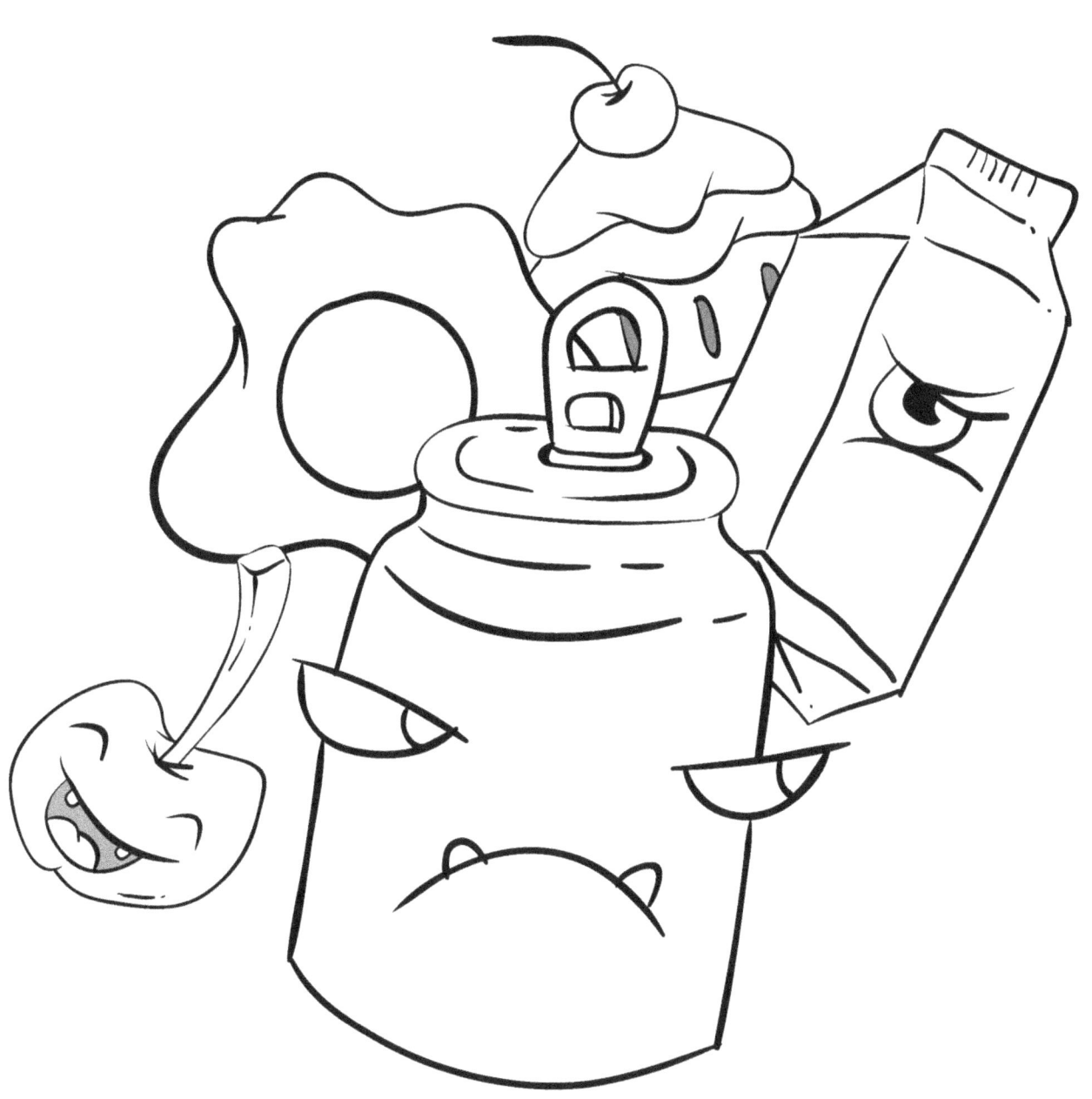

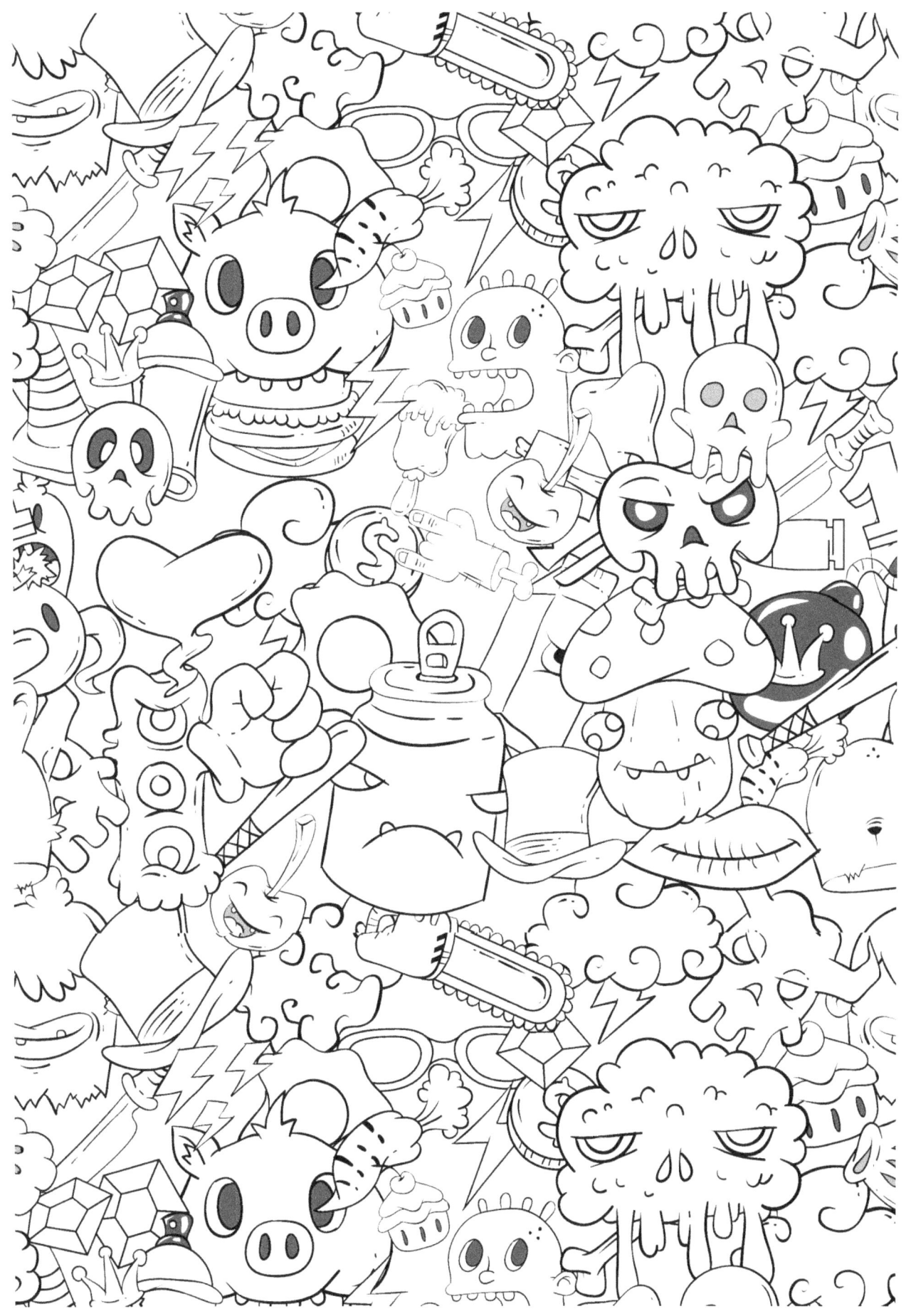

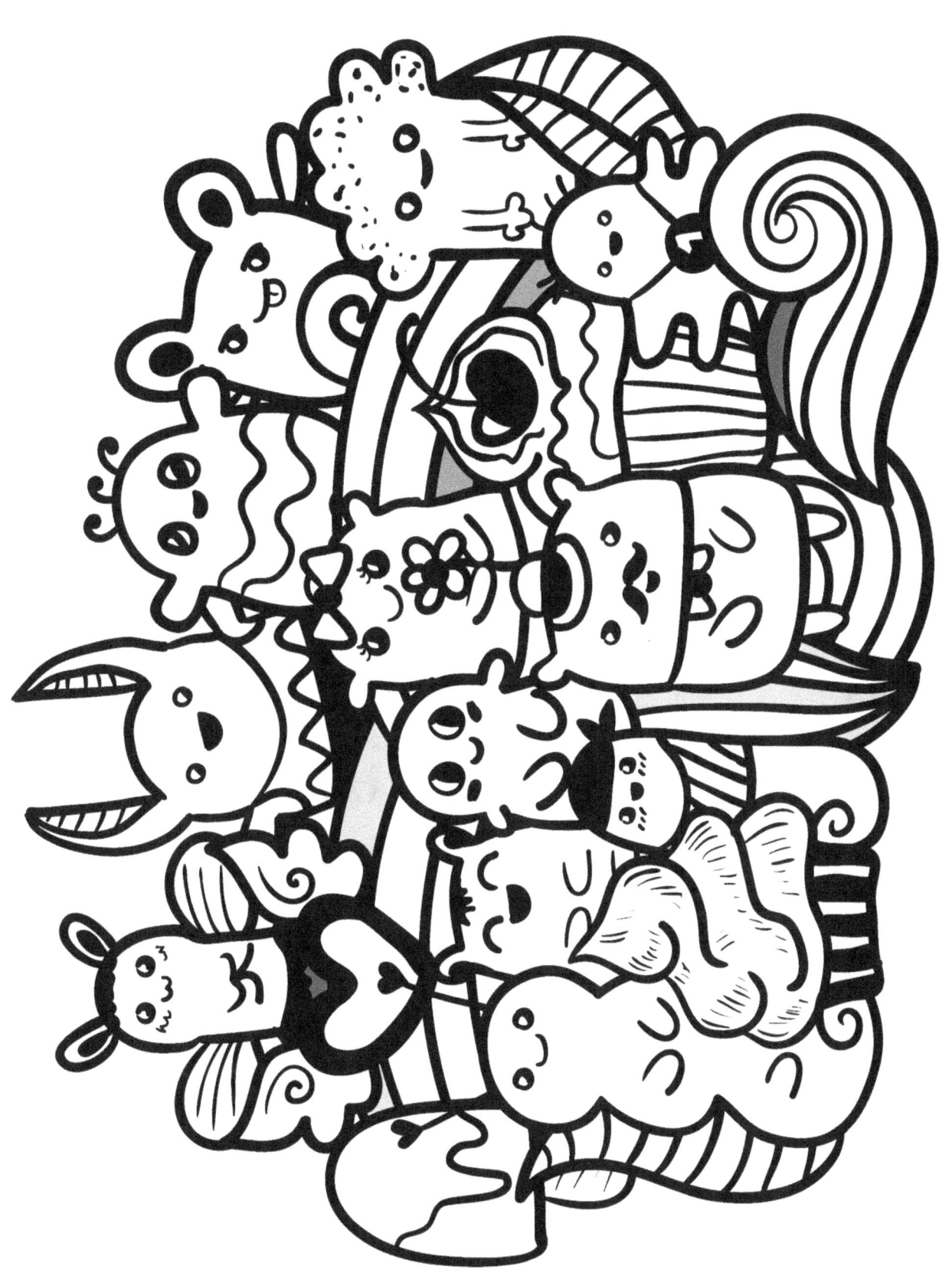

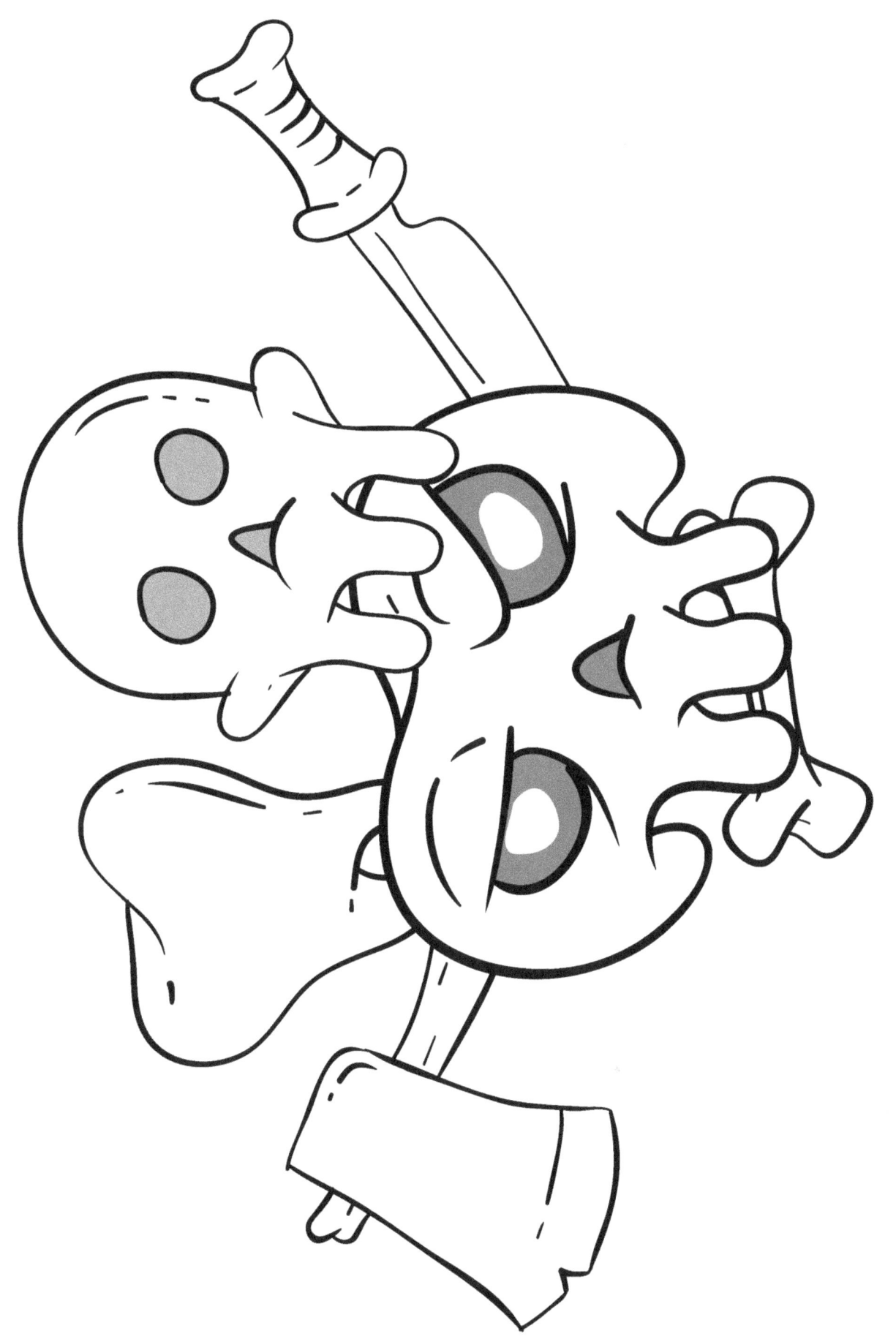

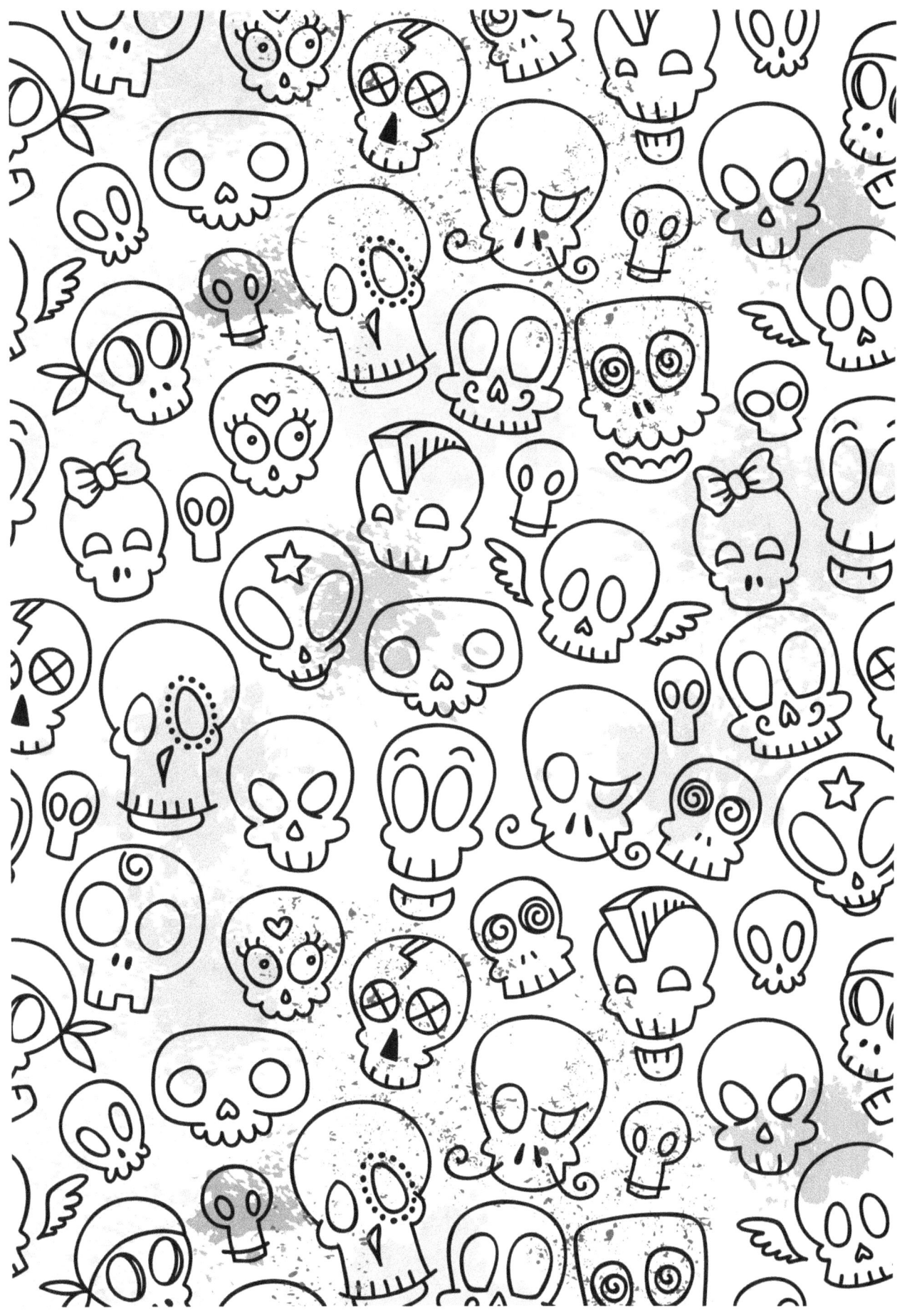

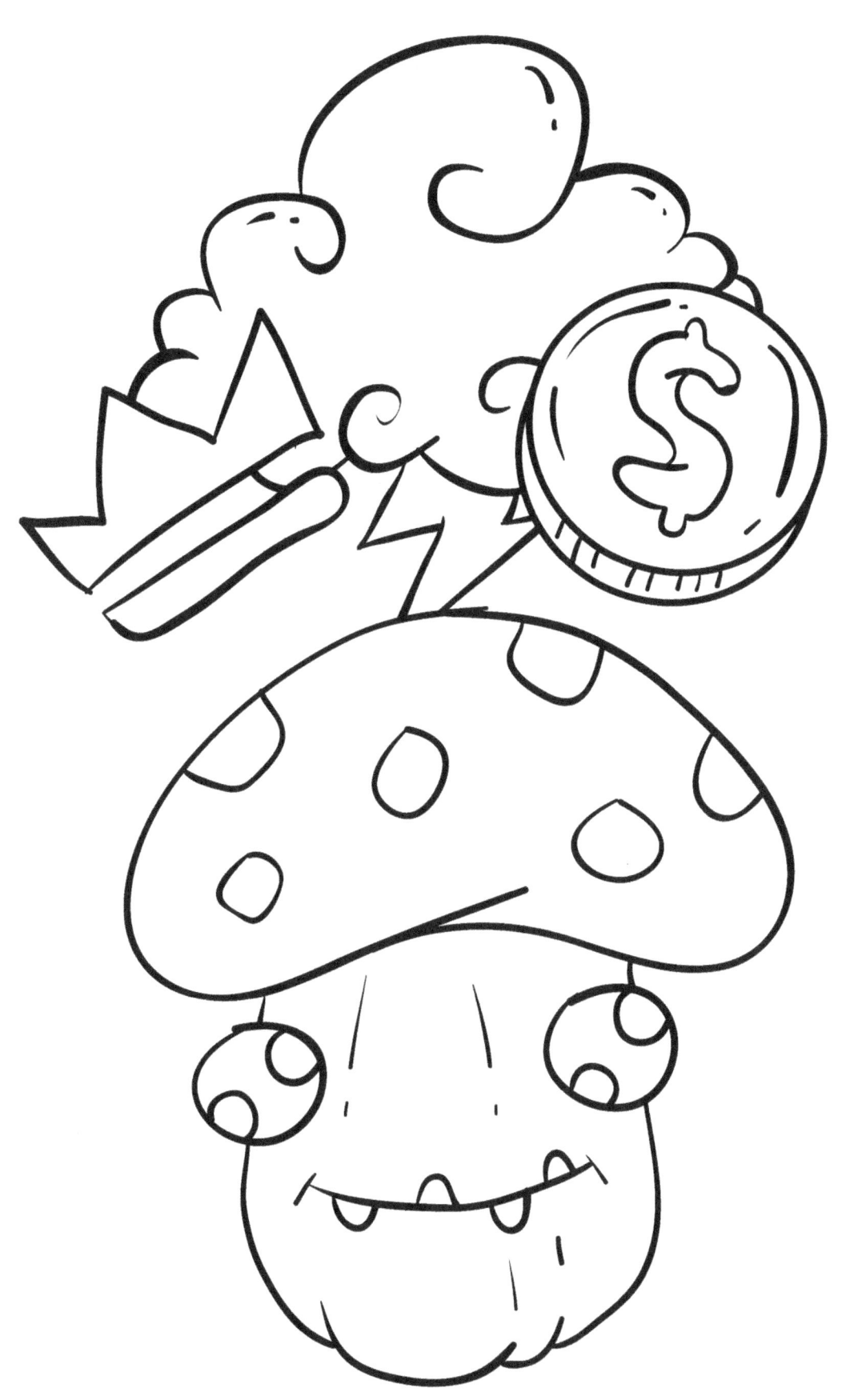

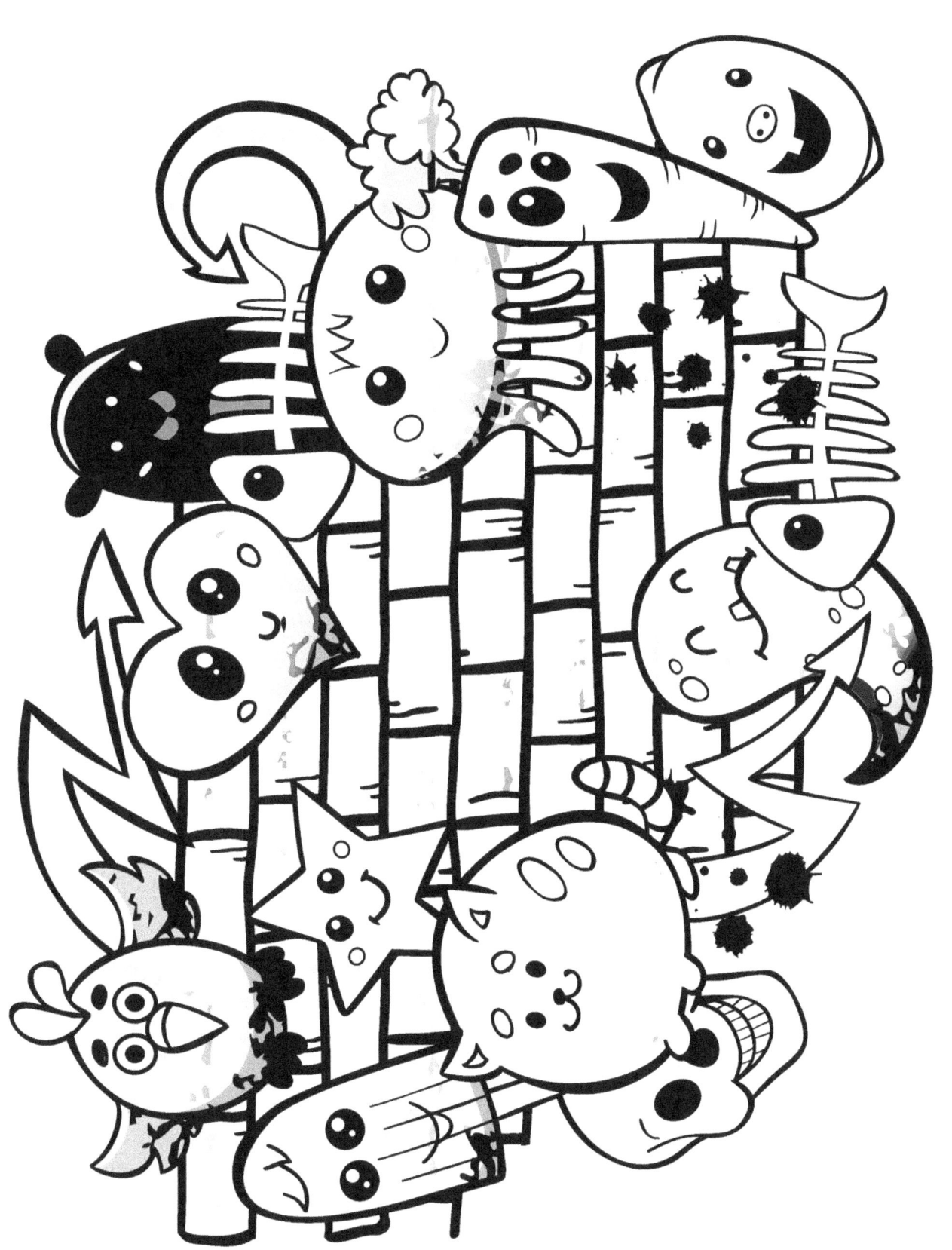

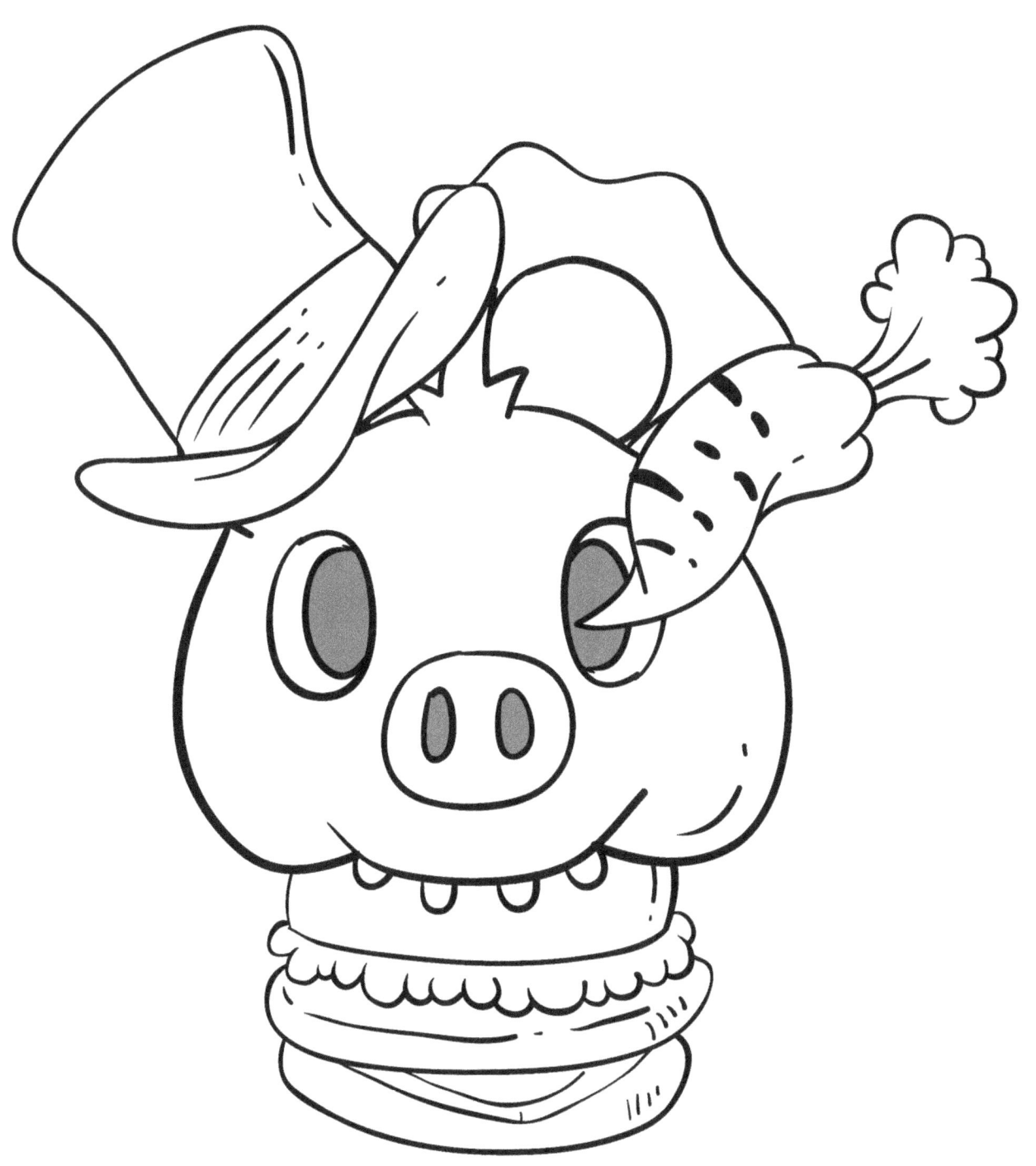

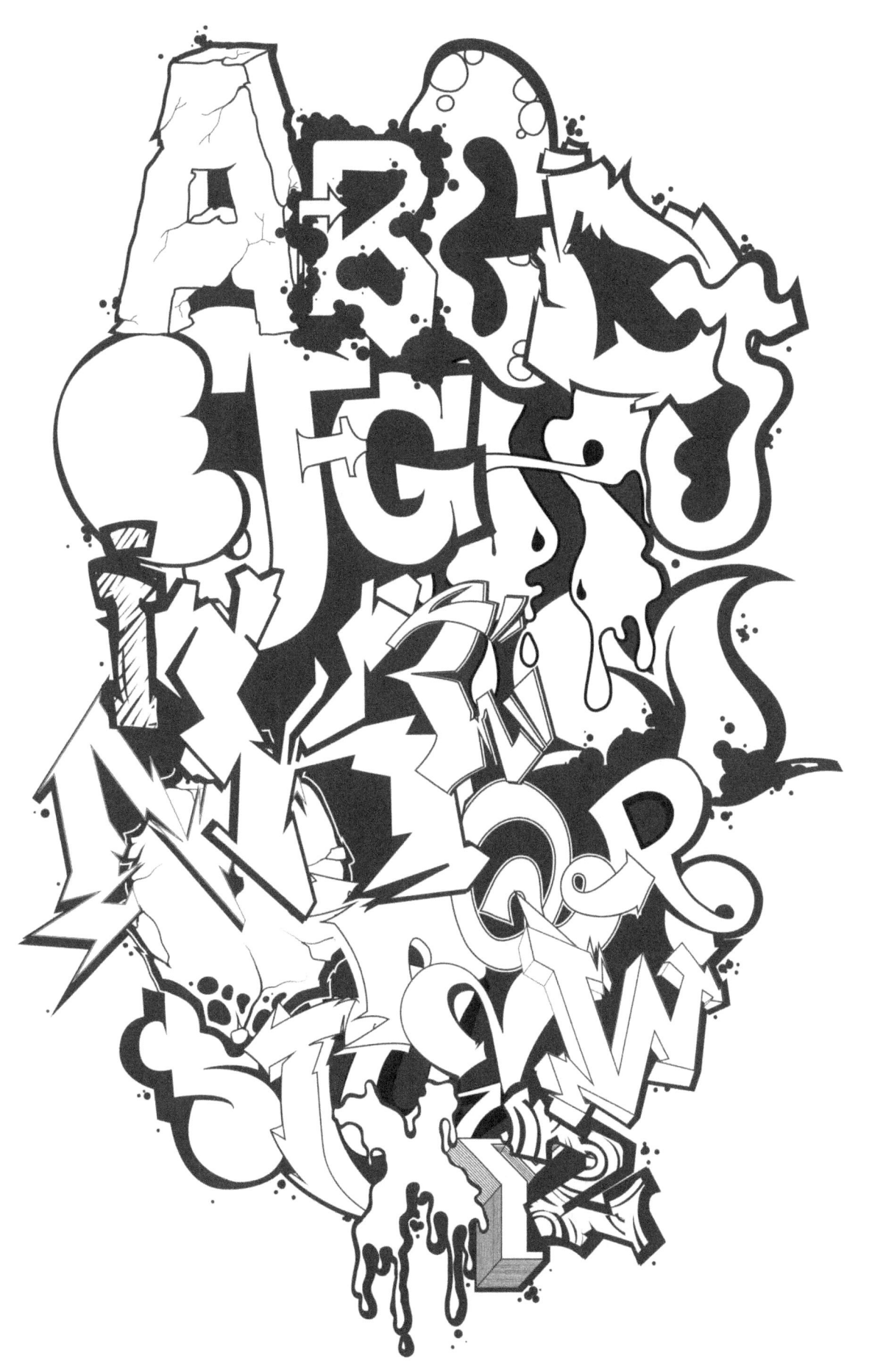

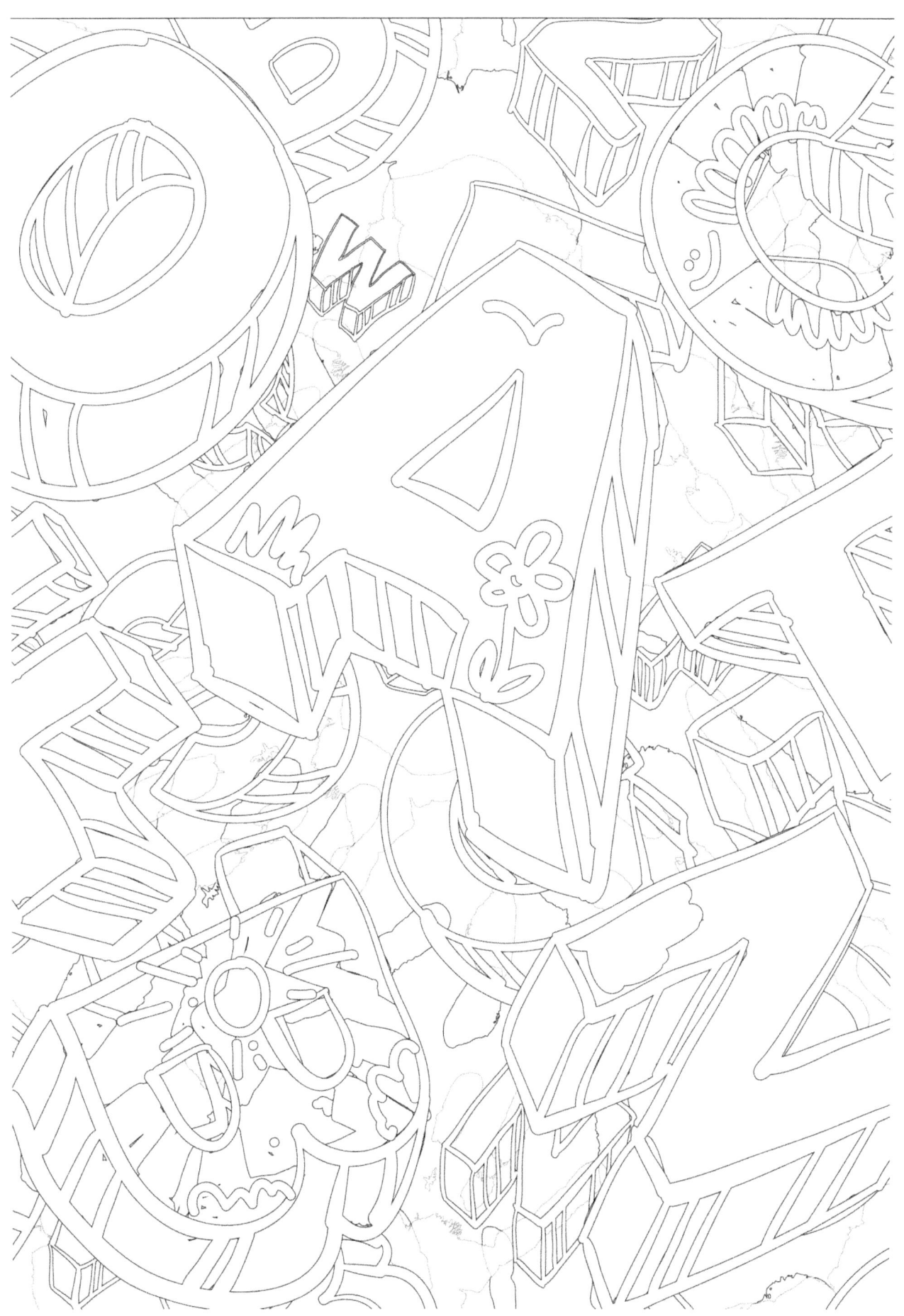

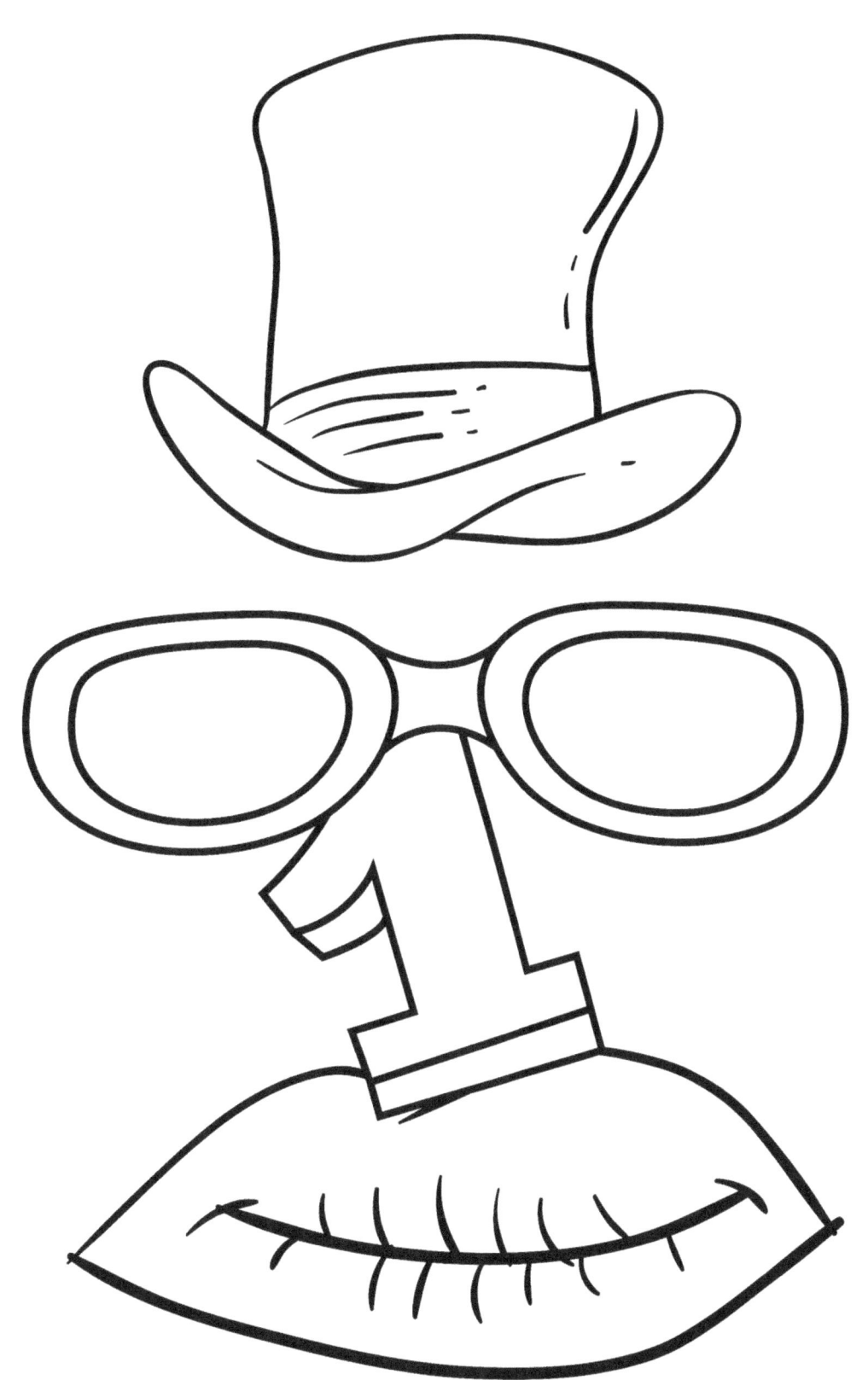

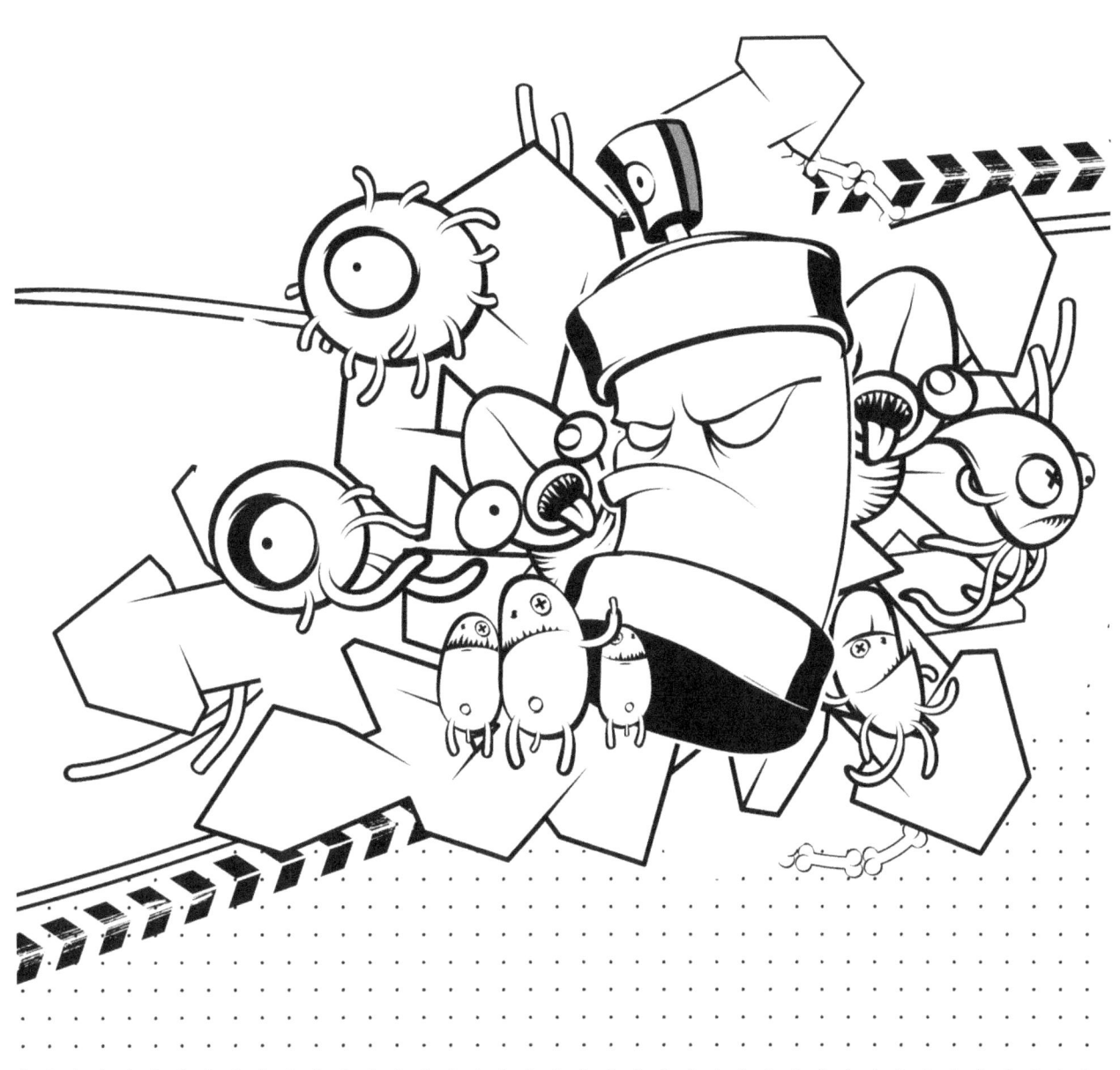

www.ingramcontent.com/pod-product-compliance
Lightning Source LLC
Chambersburg PA
CBHW081247180526
45170CB00007B/2341